Africa

by
Fran Sammis

BENCHMARK BOOKS

MARSHALL CAVENDISH
NEW YORK

Marshall Cavendish Corporation
99 White Plains Road
Tarrytown, New York 10591-9001

© Marshall Cavendish Corporation 1999

Series created by Blackbirch Graphics, Inc.

Photo Credits
Pages 13, 30, and 53: ©Y. Arthus-Bertrand/Peter Arnold; page 18: ©M.C. Denis-Huot/Peter Arnold (secretary birds) and ©A. Visage/Peter Arnold (lemurs); page 22: © IFA Bilderteam/Peter Arnold; page 34: ©Hilary Wilkes/International Stock; page 37: North Wind Picture Archives; page 45: ©Jeffrey L. Rotman/Peter Arnold; page 56: ©International Stock; page 58: ©Oldrich Karasek/Peter Arnold.

Printed in Hong Kong

Library of Congress Cataloging-in-Publication Data

Sammis, Fran.
    Africa / by Fran Sammis
        p.   cm. — (Mapping our world)
    Includes bibliographical references and index.
    Summary: Text and maps introduce information about the climate, regions, people, cultures, animals, plants, resources, politics, and religions of Africa.
    ISBN 0-7614-0372-8
    1. Cartography—Africa—Juvenile literature. [1. Cartography—Africa 2. Africa—Maps.] I. Title. II. Series: Sammis, Fran. Mapping our world.
    GA1341.S26   1998
    960—dc21   97-52590
                                                                             CIP
                                                                                  AC

Contents

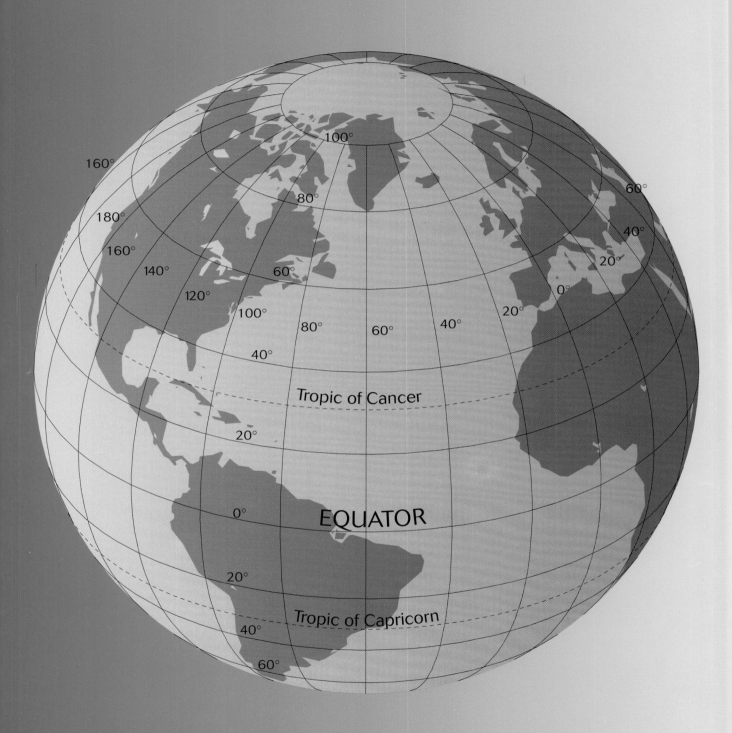

100°

160°

180°

160°

140°

120°

100°

80°

60°

40°

20°

60°

40°

20°

0°

20°

80°

60°

40°

Tropic of Cancer

20°

0°

EQUATOR

20°

Tropic of Capricorn

40°

60°

The Importance of Maps

As tools for understanding and navigating the world around us, maps are an essential resource. Maps provide us with a representation of a place, drawn or printed on a flat surface. The place that is shown may be as vast as the solar system or as small as a neighborhood park. What we learn about the place depends on the kind of map we are using.

Kinds of Maps

Physical maps show what the land itself looks like. These maps can be used to locate and identify natural geographic features such as mountains, bodies of water, deserts, and forests.

Distribution maps show where something can be found. There are two kinds of distribution maps. One shows the range or area a feature covers, such as a map showing where grizzly bears live or where hardwood forests grow.

The second kind of distribution map shows the density of a feature. That is, how much or how little of the feature is present. These maps allow us to see patterns in the way a feature is distributed. Rainfall and population maps are two examples of this kind of distribution map.

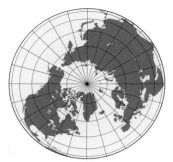
Globular

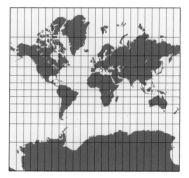
Mercator

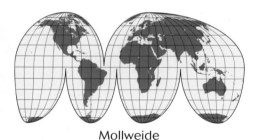
Mollweide

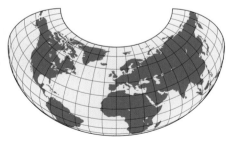
Armadillo

Political maps show us how an area is divided into countries, states, provinces, or other units. They also show where cities and towns are located. Major highways and transportation routes are also included on some kinds of political maps.

Movement maps help us find our way around. They can be road maps, street maps, and public transportation maps. Special movement maps called "charts" are used by airplane or boat pilots to navigate through air or on water.

Why Maps Are Important

Many people depend on maps to do their jobs. A geologist, for example, uses maps of Earth's structure to locate natural resources such as coal or petroleum. A transportation planner will use population maps to determine where new roads may need to be built.

A map can tell us how big a place is, where one place is in relation to another, what a place was like in the past, and what it's like now. Maps help us understand and move through our own part of the world and the rest of the world, too. Some maps even help us move through our solar system and universe!

Terms to Know

Maps are created and designed by incorporating many different elements and accepted cartographic (mapmaking) techniques. Often, maps showing the exact same area will differ from one another, depending upon the choice or critical elements, such as scale and projection. Following is a brief listing of some key mapmaking terms.

Projection. A projection is a way to represent the round Earth on a flat surface. There are a number of different ways to project, or transfer, round-Earth information to a flat surface, though each method results in some distortion. That is, areas may appear larger or smaller than they really are—or closer or farther apart. The maps on page 6 show a few varieties of projections.

Latitude. Lines of latitude, or parallels, run parallel to the equator (the imaginary center of Earth's circumference) and are used to locate points north and south of the equator. The equator is 0 degrees latitude, the north pole is 90 degrees north latitude, and the south pole is 90 degrees south latitude.

Longitude. Lines of longitude, or meridians, run at right angles to the equator and meet at the north and south poles. Lines of longitude are used to locate points east and west of the prime meridian.

Prime meridian. An imaginary line that runs through Greenwich, England; considered 0 degrees longitude. Lines to the west of the prime meridian go halfway around the world to 180 degrees west longitude; lines to the east go to 180 degrees east longitude.

Hemisphere. A half circle. Dividing the world in half from pole to pole along the prime meridian gives you the eastern and western hemispheres. Dividing the world in half at the equator gives you the northern and southern hemispheres.

Scale. The relationship of distance on a map to the actual distance on the ground. Scale can be expressed in three ways:

1. As a ratio—1:63,360 (one inch equals 63,360 inches)
2. Verbally—one inch equals one mile
3. Graphically— [1 mi.]

Because 63,360 inches equal one mile, these scales give the same information: one map-inch equals one mile on the ground.

Large-scale maps show a small area, such as a city park, in great detail. Small-scale maps show a large area, such as an entire continent, in much less detail, and on a much smaller scale.

The Art and Process of Mapmaking

Maps have been made for thousands of years. Early maps, based on first-hand exploration, were some of the most accurate tools of their

◀◀ *Opposite: The maps shown here are just four of the many different projections in which the world can be displayed.*

225 million years ago

1

180 million years ago

2

65 million years ago

3

present day

4

time. Others, based on guesses about what an area was like, were often very beautiful, but were not especially accurate.

As technology—such as photography and flight—evolved, cartographers (mapmakers) were able not only to map most of Earth in detail, they were also able to make maps of our solar system.

To make a map today, cartographers first determine what a map is to show and who is most likely to use it. Then, they assemble the information they will need for the map, which can come from many different kinds of experts—such as meteorologists, geologists, and surveyors—as well as from aerial photography or satellite feedback.

Mapping a Changing Earth

If you traced around all the land masses shown on a world map, then cut them out and put them together like a jigsaw puzzle, the result would look something like map 1 at the top of this page. Scientists think this is how Earth looked about 225 million years ago.

Over time, this single continent, Pangaea (Pan–JEE–uh), slowly broke apart into two land masses called Laurasia and Gondwanaland (map 2). Maps 3 and 4 show how the land masses continued to break up and drift apart over millions of years, until the continents assumed the shapes and positions we recognize today. Earth has not, however, finished changing.

Scientists have established that Earth's surface is made up of sections called tectonic plates. These rigid plates, shown in the map on page 9, are in

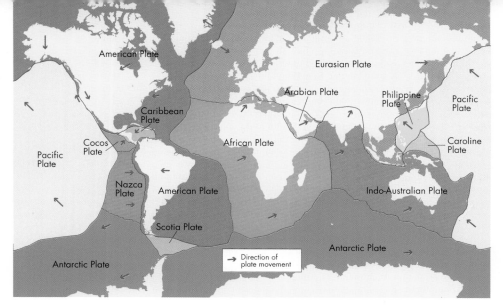

◀ *Left:* The tectonic plates that lie beneath Earth's surface are in a slow but constant motion.

◀◀ *Opposite:* The continents of our planet were once clumped together but have spread apart over millions of years in what is called continental drift.

slow, constant motion, moving from 1/4 to 1 inch a year. As they move, they take the continents and sea floors with them. Sometimes, their movements cause disasters, such as earthquakes and volcanic activity.

After many more millions of years have passed, our earth's continents will again look very different from what we know today.

Reading a Map

In order for a map to be useful, it must be the right kind of map for the job. A small-scale map of Illinois would not help you find your way around Chicago; for that, you would need a large-scale map of the city. A physical map of North America would not tell you where most of the people live; you would need a distribution map that shows population.

Once you have found the right map, you will need to refer to the map legend, or key, to be sure you are interpreting the map's information correctly. Depending on the type of map, the legend tells the scale used for the map, and notes the meaning of any symbols and colors used.

In their most basic form, maps function as place finders. They show us where places are, and we use these maps to keep from getting lost. But as you have begun to see, maps can tell us much more about our world than simply where places are located. Just how much more, you'll discover in the chapters ahead.

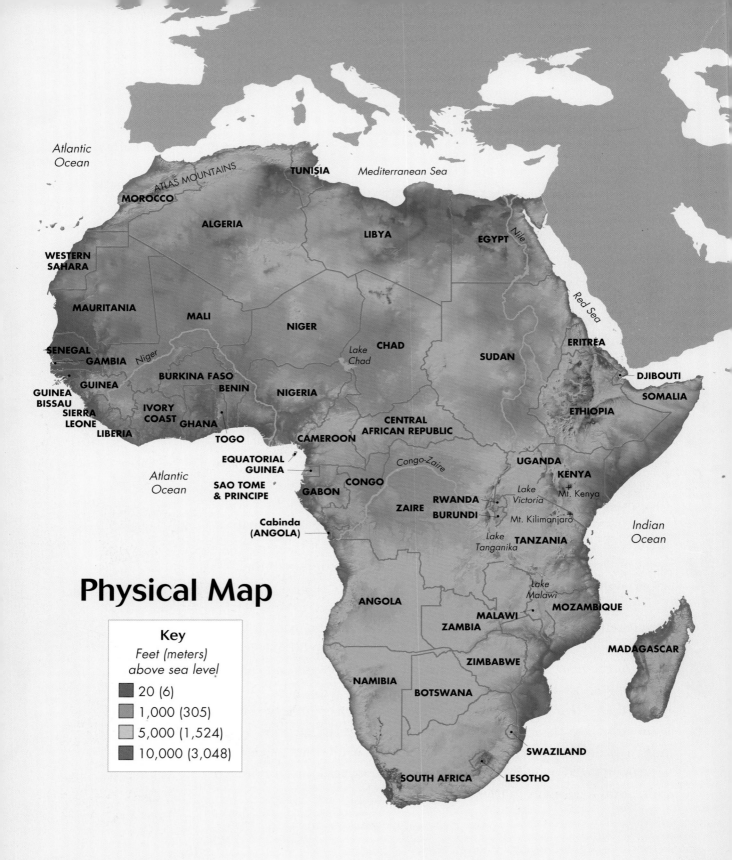

Physical Map

Atlantic Ocean

ATLAS MOUNTAINS
MOROCCO
TUNISIA
Mediterranean Sea
ALGERIA
LIBYA
EGYPT
Nile
WESTERN SAHARA
Red Sea
MAURITANIA
MALI
NIGER
CHAD
SUDAN
ERITREA
Lake Chad
DJIBOUTI
SENEGAL
Niger
GAMBIA
BURKINA FASO
SOMALIA
GUINEA
BENIN
GUINEA BISSAU
NIGERIA
CENTRAL AFRICAN REPUBLIC
ETHIOPIA
SIERRA LEONE
IVORY COAST
LIBERIA
GHANA
TOGO
CAMEROON
UGANDA
KENYA
EQUATORIAL GUINEA
Congo-Zaire
Lake Victoria
Mt. Kenya
Atlantic Ocean
SAO TOME & PRINCIPE
GABON
CONGO
ZAIRE
RWANDA
BURUNDI
Mt. Kilimanjaro
Cabinda (ANGOLA)
Lake Tanganika
TANZANIA
Indian Ocean
Lake Malawi
ANGOLA
MOZAMBIQUE
MALAWI
ZAMBIA
MADAGASCAR
ZIMBABWE
NAMIBIA
BOTSWANA
SWAZILAND
SOUTH AFRICA
LESOTHO

Key
Feet (meters) above sea level

- 20 (6)
- 1,000 (305)
- 5,000 (1,524)
- 10,000 (3,048)

Mapping Natural Zones and Regions

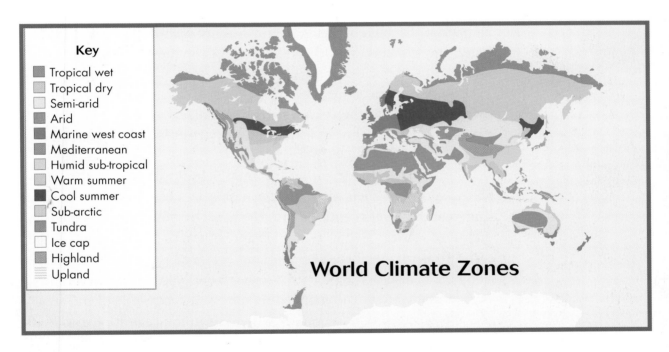

Key

- Tropical wet
- Tropical dry
- Semi-arid
- Arid
- Marine west coast
- Mediterranean
- Humid sub-tropical
- Warm summer
- Cool summer
- Sub-arctic
- Tundra
- Ice cap
- Highland
- Upland

World Climate Zones

Africa is the second-largest continent in the world. It covers enough space to contain three land areas the size of the United States, with room to spare. Measuring across Africa from its bulge on the west to its "horn" on the east (in Somalia), the continent is nearly as wide as it is long: 4,700 miles (7,563 kilometers) from west to east and 5,000 miles (8,046 kilometers) from north to south.

▲ *Above: As this climate map shows, some of the most arid (dry) regions of the world are in Africa.*

◄◄ *Opposite: Africa is ringed by a narrow coastal plain, colored dark green on the map.*

To learn about what Africa is like, you might start by referring to maps that show its physical features (topography), climate, land use, and other natural characteristics.

Africa's Topography

Today, Africa's interior physical features are well known—and accurately mapped—thanks in large part to European explorers who penetrated the interior of the continent during the eighteenth and nineteenth centuries.

Before then, only the coastline of Africa and North Africa were familiar to Europeans. The northern portions of Africa had been mapped since ancient times by inhabitants such as the Egyptians. Later, the Romans and others involved in conquest or trade added information about the area.

Portuguese navigators began exploring Africa's coast in the 1300s. By the early 1500s, the coastal areas were fairly well mapped. Africa's interior, especially the land south of the Sahara Desert, was another matter.

Here, cartographers either invented people, places, and things to fill the spaces on their maps, or they left spaces blank. When the first European explorers ventured into the heart of Africa and reported on their discoveries, they were not always believed. For example, in the early 1770s, James Bruce of Scotland explored present-day Ethiopia along the course of the Blue Nile—one of the Nile River's two branches. He reported on and mapped the physical geography of the area and also wrote about the people who lived in the region. Bruce described huge Ethiopian armies, and unusual food customs that people found too fantastic to believe. As a result, they thought his maps were not realistic. It was not until after Bruce died in 1794 that other explorers proved the accuracy of Bruce's maps and descriptions.

Looking at the physical map of Africa on page 10, you can see that the majority of the continent is a plateau that drops sharply on most sides to narrow coastal plains. In the far northeast, across

Morocco, Algeria, and Tunisia, lie the Atlas Mountains. Other mountains are found along eastern Africa's Great Rift Valley, which runs from Eritrea to Tanzania and Mozambique. Mt. Kilimanjaro and Mt. Kenya—the first- and second-highest mountains in Africa—are located there.

The Rift Valley is also home to the world's longest freshwater lake, Lake Tanganyika, which forms part of the border with Tanzania. Lake Victoria, part of which is in northern Tanzania, is Africa's largest lake and the second-largest freshwater lake in the world.

Several of the world's major rivers are in Africa. The Nile, the longest river in the world, is 4,180 miles (6,727 kilometers). It flows from Lake Victoria north to the Mediterranean Sea. Other important rivers include the Congo-Zaire and the Niger, Africa's second- and third-longest rivers.

▼ *Below: This section of the Great Rift Valley lies in Kenya.*

Climate and Weather

Africa's physical traits are affected by its climate. Climate and weather are not the same thing. Weather is short-lived; it changes from day to day. Climate is the average characteristics of the weather in a given place over a long period of time. Although climates can change, they do so much more slowly than weather—over many years, rather than days.

Meteorologists use a variety of high-tech methods to gather the information that allows them to analyze and predict the weather. Among those methods are sophisticated ways of viewing and mapping the world.

Analyzing and Predicting Weather

The major elements that are used to describe the weather and categorize climate are: temperature, precipitation, humidity, amount of sunshine, wind, and air pressure.

Manned and unmanned weather stations on land and at sea, weather balloons, airplanes, and satellites are all used in gathering weather information for analysis. Radar, cameras, and thermal infrared sensors monitor and record the weather conditions.

The information from these sources is sent to weather centers throughout the world by means of a worldwide satellite system, called the Global Telecommunications System (GTS). The information is fed into computers that record and analyze the data, which can then be compiled into highly detailed and informative maps. The GTS also allows weather centers to share their data.

By studying global weather patterns over a long time, climatologists can map climatic regions—areas that have similar climates. The world climate map on page 11 is just one example of this kind of map.

Africa's Climate

Africa is divided in half by the equator. This means the land area in each half is roughly the same distance from the equator. This, in turn, means the northern and southern halves contain similar climate regions. About 75 percent of Africa lies within tropical climate zones.

▶▶ *Opposite: This climate map of Africa shows that most of the continent is in either a tropical or an arid zone.*

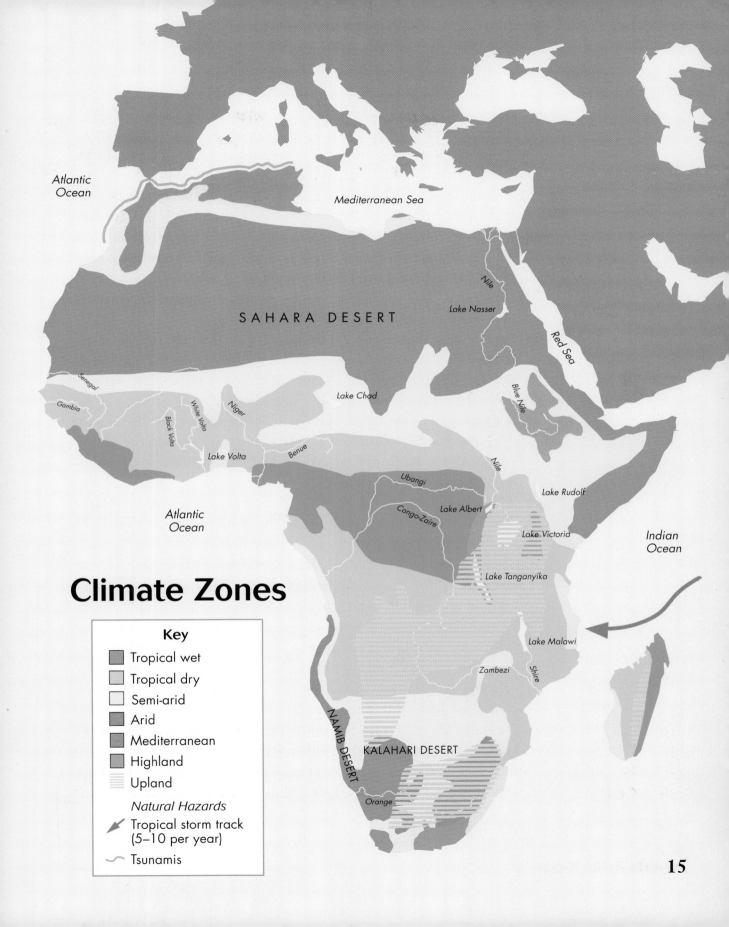

Climate Zones

Key

- ◼ Tropical wet
- ◻ Tropical dry
- ◻ Semi-arid
- ◼ Arid
- ◼ Mediterranean
- ◼ Highland
- ▦ Upland

Natural Hazards

- ↙ Tropical storm track (5–10 per year)
- ⌇ Tsunamis

Atlantic Ocean

Mediterranean Sea

SAHARA DESERT

Nile

Lake Nasser

Red Sea

Senegal

Gambia

White Volta

Black Volta

Niger

Lake Chad

Blue Nile

Lake Volta

Benue

Nile

Atlantic Ocean

Ubangi

Congo-Zaire

Lake Albert

Lake Rudolf

Lake Victoria

Lake Tanganyika

Indian Ocean

Lake Malawi

NAMIB DESERT

Zambezi

Shire

KALAHARI DESERT

Orange

15

The temperature is therefore fairly consistent—generally warm or hot—throughout the continent. The biggest variation is in rainfall. Looking at the climate map on page 15, you can see that Africa includes a number of climate variations. However, six major climate regions exist on the continent, each with distinctive rainfall patterns.

- Along the equator, in the western and central parts of Africa, rainfall is heavy and consistent throughout the year. This is the tropical wet region (colored deep green on the map), where the rain forests are located. It is the largest rain forest area outside of the Amazon, in South America.
- Surrounding that region are tropical dry areas where rainfall is seasonal. These are the savanna, or grassland, regions. There, both wet and dry seasons occur. During the wet season (some areas have two wet seasons) rainfall is quite heavy.
- Semi-arid areas with light and irregular rainfall border the deserts: the Sahara in the north, the Kalahari in the south, and the Namib Desert along the southwest coast. The semi-arid areas are sometimes referred to as the steppes.
- The arid deserts, colored red on the climate map, are very dry. The Sahara—the largest desert in the world—and the Namib receive an average rainfall of less than 10 inches a year. In the Sahara, most of this moisture is concentrated at the northern and southern edges. Interior portions of the Sahara may go for years without any rainfall at all.
- Hot, dry summers and mild winters with moderate precipitation make up a Mediterranean climate, colored blue on the map. As the name implies, this kind of climate is found along parts of the African coast bordering the Mediterranean Sea. The same kind of climate is also found in the very far southwestern part of Africa, in the area of Cape Town, South Africa.
- Highland areas are found mainly in East Africa. Because of their altitude, highland areas tend to be cooler and wetter than the savanna area that often surrounds the highlands.

Animals and Plants

Thousands of different animal and plant species inhabit Africa's climate zones. Before the interior of the continent was fully explored, map-makers illustrated maps of Africa with strange, imaginary animals, which they placed alongside pictures of known animals. Now, even without these imaginary beasts, the animals of the African savanna are a tourist attraction worldwide.

The rain forest areas provide a home to chimpanzees, many different monkey species, bats, okapi, and gorillas. Snakes, lizards, frogs, and toads also inhabit these areas; crocodiles and hippopotamuses are found in rivers and swamps. There, you will also find the famous Goliath frog, the world's largest frog, which can weigh as much as seven pounds (3.17 kilograms)!

Many different birds are also found in the rain forest, including parrots, kingfishers, and hornbills.

Oil palms; hardwood trees such as mahogany, teak, and ebony; the softwood tree okoume, and fruit trees are found throughout the forest. Mangrove trees are found in swampy areas.

The savanna, or grasslands (the tropical dry areas on the climate map on page 15), provide a home for an astonishing variety of large animals that tourists from around the world come to see. Antelopes ranging in size from 15-inch-(.38 centimeter) high dik-diks (the smallest of all antelopes) to 6-foot-(1.8 meter) tall, 1,500-pound (680-kilogram) elands roam the grasslands. Other animals of the savanna include wildebeests (gnus), warthogs, gazelles, giraffes, zebras, rhinoceros, elephants, baboons, and anteaters. The swiftest predators of the savanna include lions, cheetahs, leopards, African wild dogs, hyenas, and jackals.

Bird species are especially abundant in the savanna regions. There, you can see everything from common birds such as eagles, hawks, ducks, and geese, to more exotic birds such as storks, secretary birds, and ostriches. The lakes of East Africa (see the topographical map on page 10) are home to an amazing number of flamingos, as well as

▲◀ Above left: Secretary birds, such as this pair, are at home on the savanna.

▲▶ Above right: These lemurs live in Madagascar, which has some of the richest plant and animal life in the world.

cranes, ibises, cormorants, and anhingas. Vultures keep an eye on the hunters of the savanna, waiting to pick the remains of their prey.

Grasses cover the savanna; short, sparse grass is predominant in the dry areas near the deserts, and taller, denser grass is found in the areas near forests that receive more rain. Trees such as the baobab and the acacia, or thorn tree, and various hardy shrubs are also found scattered throughout the savanna regions.

The deserts provide homes for animals such as fennec foxes, jerboas (which look rather like large gerbils), rabbits, and weasel-like meerkats, as well as small insects such as beetles.

Succulents—water-storing plants such as cacti and, on the oases, date palms—are among the relatively few plants found in the desert regions.

The Mediterranean areas of Africa house animals that are very similar to those of southern Europe and southwest Asia. There you can find the Barbary ape and African red deer, as well as the antelope-like ibex.

Plants found in these areas include cork, cedar, and olive trees, as well as evergreen bushes such as myrtle, and grape vines.

When it comes to animals and plants, the island of Madagascar rates a special mention. Madagascar, off the east coast of Africa, is one of only two places in the world where you can find true lemurs, which are small primates. The other place is Africa's Cormoros Islands.

In addition, the coelacanth (SEA-la-canth), an ancient "living fossil" fish, is found in the waters off Madagascar. Of the many different plants on the island, the Madagascar periwinkle is especially interesting. This small plant contains material that is useful in cancer treatments.

How Climate and Topography Affect People

As we have seen, climate greatly affects plant and animal life. Of course, a region's climate and topography can affect many aspects of human life as well. Among them:

Population distribution. More people tend to settle in areas that have a mild or moderate climate, adequate rainfall, and fairly level, open land. Population will be less densely distributed in regions that are mountainous or thickly forested, and in regions with climates that are very cold or dry. You can see this connection if you compare the world climate map on page 11 in this chapter with the world population density map on page 33.

How people live and work. The type of housing people live in, the clothes they wear, and the kind of work they do, all depend in part on the climate of their region. The physical structure of the land also can affect what work people do. For example, large-scale farming is an option in plains areas, but not in mountain regions.

Agriculture. To a large extent, climate dictates what crops can or can't be successfully grown in an area. Using technology such as artificial irrigation or greenhouses can change the impact of weather and climate to a degree. However, agriculture is most successful when crops are naturally suited to the area in which they are grown.

Transportation. An area's climate and topography can dictate which forms of transportation are used there. For example, dogsleds are an obvious choice in arctic areas, while camels or elephants are well suited to travel in hot, arid conditions. More roads and railroads are built in areas that have a level terrain, as opposed to mountainous areas.

Economy. Some areas, such as deserts, have little or no natural resources. These areas have a climate or topography that doesn't allow for extensive agriculture or a developed transportation system. Such harsh regions are likely to be poorer than areas that can support industry, large-scale agriculture, or other means of making a living and engaging in trade.

The Land of Africa and Its People

By looking carefully at the land use map on the opposite page and comparing it to the climate map on page 15, you can see how Africans have adapted to their natural surroundings. For example, they raise cattle almost exclusively in the savanna, or tropical dry areas. This did not happen by chance.

In the wet tropical areas, where rainfall is abundant and consistent throughout the year, crops can easily be grown. This encouraged the establishment of settled farming communities centered on crop cultivation. Unfortunately, that same climate is also a breeding ground for insects—including the tsetse fly, whose bite is fatal to cattle. As a result, cattle-raising societies moved on to the drier areas of the savanna, where the tsetse fly wasn't a problem. And, because of the seasonal rainfall in the savanna, herders developed a nomadic, rather than a settled, lifestyle, moving about seasonally to find food and water for their cattle.

The Land of Africa and the Economy

Although cattle and sheep are valued in Africa, the land itself is the continent's most valuable resource. For all the products it provides to the economy—both mineral and agricultural—the land is the foundation of Africa.

▶▶ *Opposite: Many of the crops shown on this map are grown by Africans for home consumption.*

Agriculture is an important part of the African economy (as you can see on the land use map), since approximately two thirds of the population lives in rural areas. The majority of the cultivated land, around 60 percent, is used for subsistence farming—growing crops for personal use only. You can tell which crops are best suited to a particular climate by looking at the climate and land use maps together.

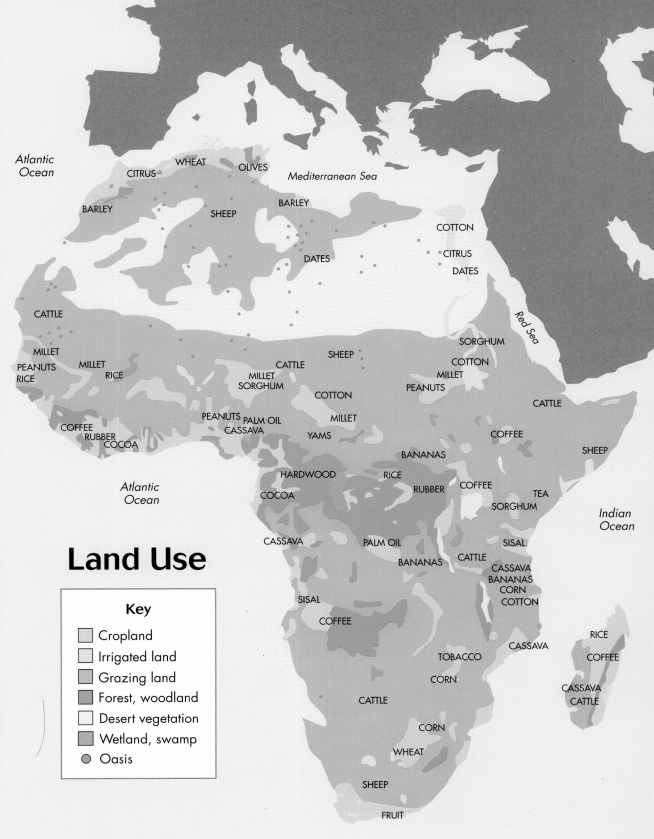

Atlantic
Ocean

WHEAT
CITRUS
OLIVES
Mediterranean Sea
BARLEY
BARLEY
SHEEP
DATES
COTTON
CITRUS
DATES
Red Sea
CATTLE
MILLET
PEANUTS
RICE
MILLET
RICE
SHEEP
CATTLE
MILLET
SORGHUM
COTTON
MILLET
SORGHUM
COTTON
MILLET
PEANUTS
CATTLE
COFFEE
RUBBER
COCOA
PEANUTS
CASSAVA
PALM OIL
YAMS
MILLET
COFFEE
SHEEP
Atlantic
Ocean
HARDWOOD
COCOA
RICE
RUBBER
BANANAS
COFFEE
TEA
SORGHUM
Indian
Ocean
CASSAVA
PALM OIL
BANANAS
SISAL
CATTLE
CASSAVA
BANANAS
CORN
COTTON
SISAL
COFFEE
CASSAVA
RICE
COFFEE
TOBACCO
CORN
CASSAVA
CATTLE
CATTLE
CORN
WHEAT
SHEEP
FRUIT

Land Use

Key

- ▢ Cropland
- ▢ Irrigated land
- ▢ Grazing land
- ▢ Forest, woodland
- ▢ Desert vegetation
- ▢ Wetland, swamp
- ● Oasis

Subsistence Crops

In the wet tropical areas of western and central Africa, bananas, plantains (a type of cooking banana), and root crops such as yams, cassava, and sweet potatoes are important subsistence food crops.

Grains such as wheat and barley are grown in northern Africa, along the Mediterranean. Other Mediterranean produce, such as olives and citrus fruits, are also grown in irrigated areas of northern Africa.

On the oases of the Sahara, farmers grow dates. South of the Sahara, in the grasslands regions of equatorial, eastern, and southern Africa, corn, millet, and sorghum are important subsistence crops. Rice is grown in the tropical wet areas of western Africa, and is also a major crop on the island country of Madagascar.

Cash Crops

Although much of Africa's agricultural production is for the farmers' own use, many farmers also grow cash crops. In some areas, huge plantations are devoted solely to growing crops for export.

Important African cash crops include cocoa (Ghana), coffee (East Africa), peanuts (West and Equatorial Africa), palm oil and palm kernels (West Africa and Equatorial Africa), tea (East Africa), and cloves (Madagascar and Tanzania). Rubber is Liberia's main cash crop. Cotton is grown in the Nile delta, and East Africa is the leading producer of sisal, which is used to make rope. Hardwoods are becoming an increasingly important export, but the harvesting of trees is also contributing to the destruction of the rain forest.

Mineral Resources

Looking at the mineral resources map on the opposite page, you can see that Africa's resources are not distributed evenly throughout the continent.

▶▶ *Opposite: The symbols clumped near the bottom of this map show that many valuable minerals are mined in southern Africa.*

▼ *Below: Cotton is harvested in Nigeria.*

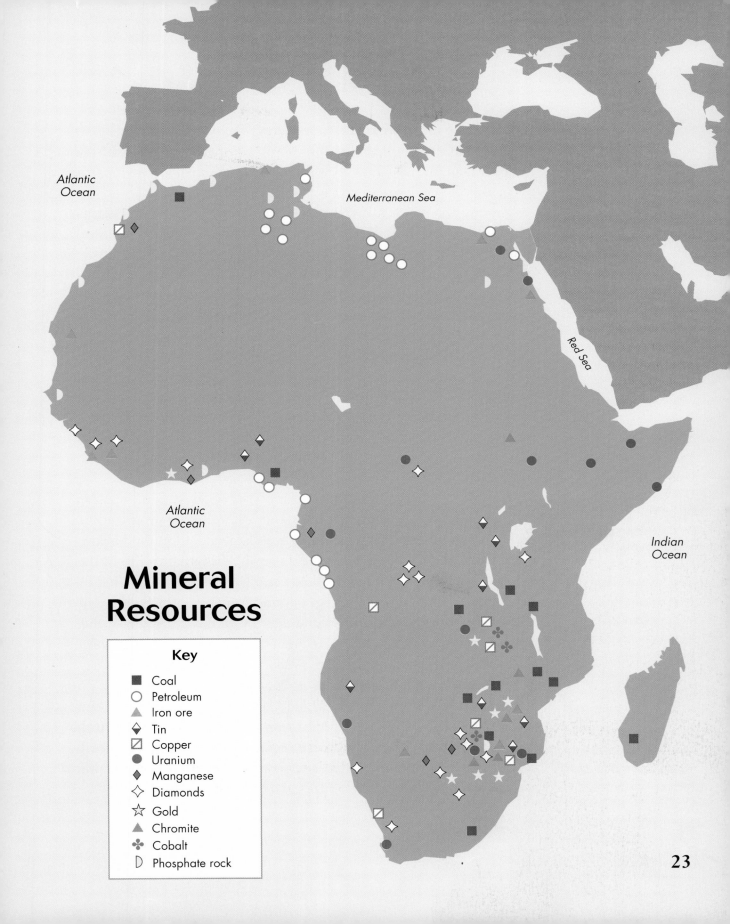

Mineral
Resources

Atlantic
Ocean

Mediterranean Sea

Red Sea

Atlantic
Ocean

Indian
Ocean

Key

- ■ Coal
- ○ Petroleum
- ▲ Iron ore
- ◆ Tin
- ▨ Copper
- ● Uranium
- ◆ Manganese
- ◇ Diamonds
- ☆ Gold
- ▲ Chromite
- ♣ Cobalt
- ⌂ Phosphate rock

23

Rather, these minerals are clustered along the north and west coastal areas, and in the southern region. If you compare this map with the political map on page 32, you will see which nations possess a particular mineral.

Among the major mineral-producing countries is South Africa, which is the world's leading gold and gem-quality diamond producer. South Africa is also a leading producer of manganese and chromite.

Libya and Algeria in the north, as well as Nigeria, are leading petroleum oil producers. Northern Africa also has major reserves of phosphate—a primary ingredient in fertilizer.

Africa as a whole produces the majority of the world's cobalt. Within the continent, Zambia is a major producer of both cobalt and copper. Uranium is important to South Africa, Namibia, Niger, and Gabon, as is tin to Zaire and Nigeria. In addition, iron ore and coal reserves in South Africa and Zimbabwe contribute to those countries' iron and steel industry, since coal is needed for the smelting process.

Energy Production and Consumption

Looking at the energy production map on the opposite page, you can see that gas and oil are the primary sources of energy produced in Africa. Natural gas fields are found heavily clustered in the Sahara, in Egypt around the Nile delta, and along the west coast north of the Congo-Zaire River. Major oil fields and basins are also located in these areas, with additional energy coming from oil basins in the Red Sea and at other points along the west-central coast. Much of the oil and gas produced in Africa is exported. Coal, found mostly in southern Africa, produces energy primarily for African industry.

The areas that consume the most energy (see the map on page 26) are northern and southern Africa, and Gabon on the west coast. Mining, industry, and oil and gas production account in large part for the heavy energy consumption in these regions. To see how Africa compares to the rest of the world in energy production and consumption, see the maps on page 27.

▶▶ *Opposite: Africa's precious gas and oil deposits are along the northern and west-central coasts.*

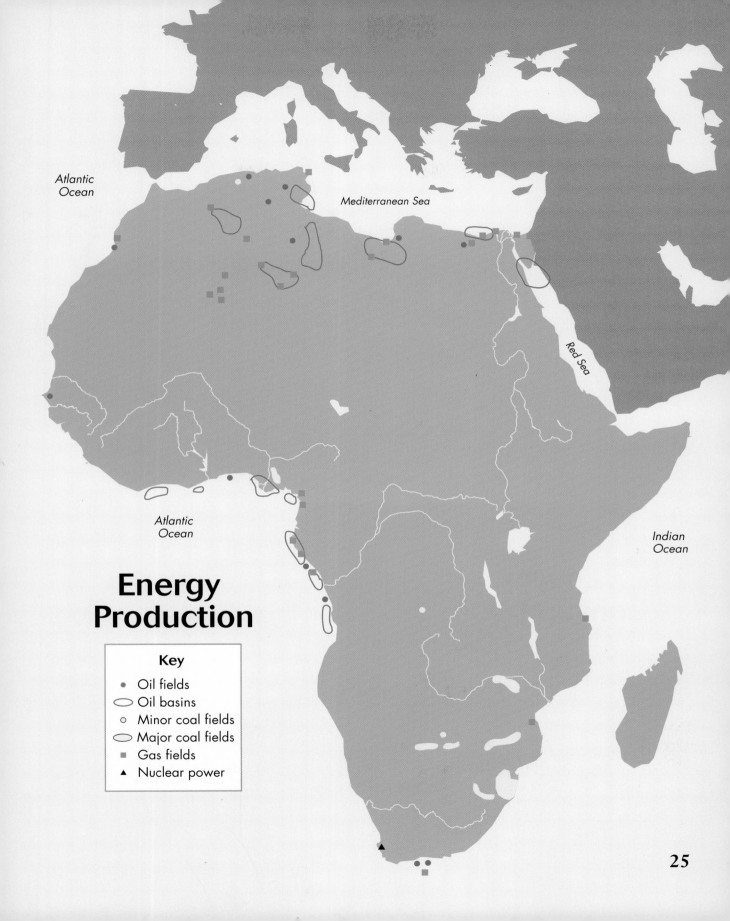

Energy
Production

Key

- ● Oil fields
- ◯ Oil basins
- ○ Minor coal fields
- ⬯ Major coal fields
- ■ Gas fields
- ▲ Nuclear power

Atlantic
Ocean

Mediterranean Sea

Red Sea

Atlantic
Ocean

Indian
Ocean

Atlantic Ocean

Mediterranean Sea

Red Sea

Atlantic Ocean

Indian Ocean

Energy Consumption

Key

☐ 0–1,000

■ 1,000–5,000

☐ Information unavailable

Consumption per capita in kilograms of coal or its equivalent (1,000 kilograms = 450 pounds)

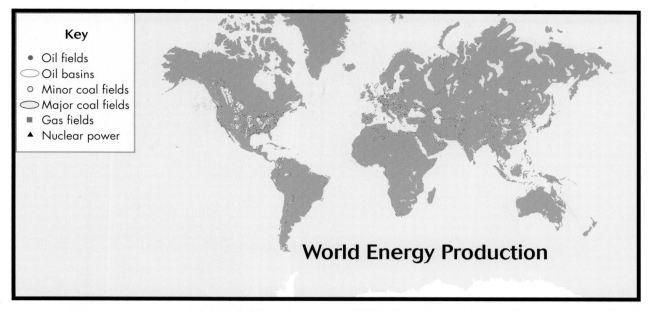

Key
- • Oil fields
- ⬭ Oil basins
- ○ Minor coal fields
- ⬭ Major coal fields
- ■ Gas fields
- ▲ Nuclear power

World Energy Production

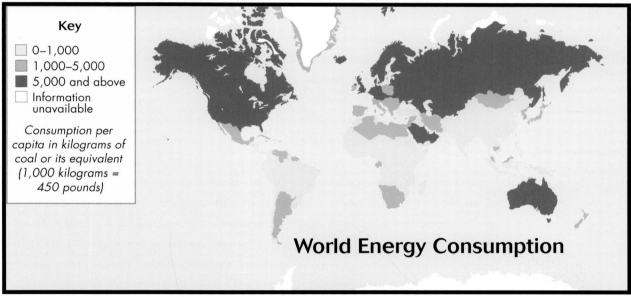

Key
- ☐ 0–1,000
- ☐ 1,000–5,000
- ☐ 5,000 and above
- ☐ Information unavailable

Consumption per capita in kilograms of coal or its equivalent (1,000 kilograms = 450 pounds)

World Energy Consumption

Finally, take a look at the map on page 28 that shows worldwide harmful emissions of fossil fuels (coal, oil, or natural gas). Here you can see how many tons of harmful substances are released into the air by the burning of coal and oil, and compare Africa to other areas of the world. Harmful emissions from the burning of fossil fuels contribute to environmental problems such as global warming, the destruction of the ozone layer, and acid rain.

▲ *Above: You can see from these maps that Africa produces and consumes a small portion of the world's supply of energy.*

◀◀ *Opposite: Energy consumption is heaviest in northern and southern Africa, where mining and gas and oil production are concentrated.*

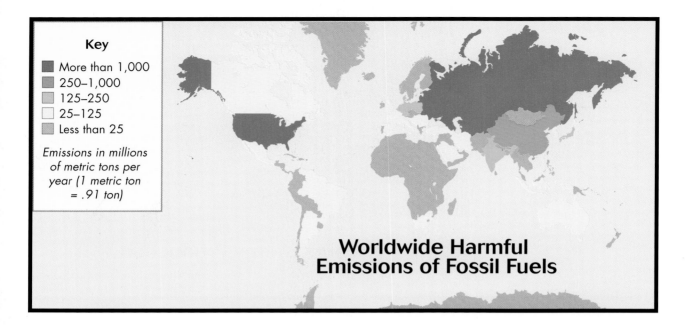

Key
■ More than 1,000
■ 250–1,000
■ 125–250
☐ 25–125
▨ Less than 25

Emissions in millions of metric tons per year (1 metric ton = .91 ton)

Worldwide Harmful Emissions of Fossil Fuels

▲ *Above: As a low producer and consumer of energy, Africa creates relatively few fossil fuel emissions.*

▶▶ *Opposite: Africa's greatest environmental problems are desertification and deforestation.*

The Environment

Africa has a relatively low level of fossil fuel emissions because it is less industrialized than many other parts of the world. Even so, industry has already begun to damage the environment. Some of this damage is shown on the map on the opposite page.

The most industrialized country on the continent is South Africa. Here, run-off from industry has contributed to the pollution of coastal waters. The coastal waters of the Nile delta and Red Sea areas of northern Egypt, as well as areas of the west-central coast of Africa, have been affected by oil and gas production, and by pollution from chemical plants. (All of this coastal pollution is indicated in purple on the map.) In addition, increased mining efforts throughout Africa are contributing to deforestation and erosion. In the worst cases, this has led to desertification—fertile land turning to desert. You can examine the connections between mining, energy production, and environmental damage by comparing the environmental damage map with the energy production map on page 25 and the mineral resources map on page 23.

The lumber industry has had a devastating effect on the African rain forest. Trees in central West Africa (marked "hardwood" on the map on page 21) have been cut with little thought given to replanting.

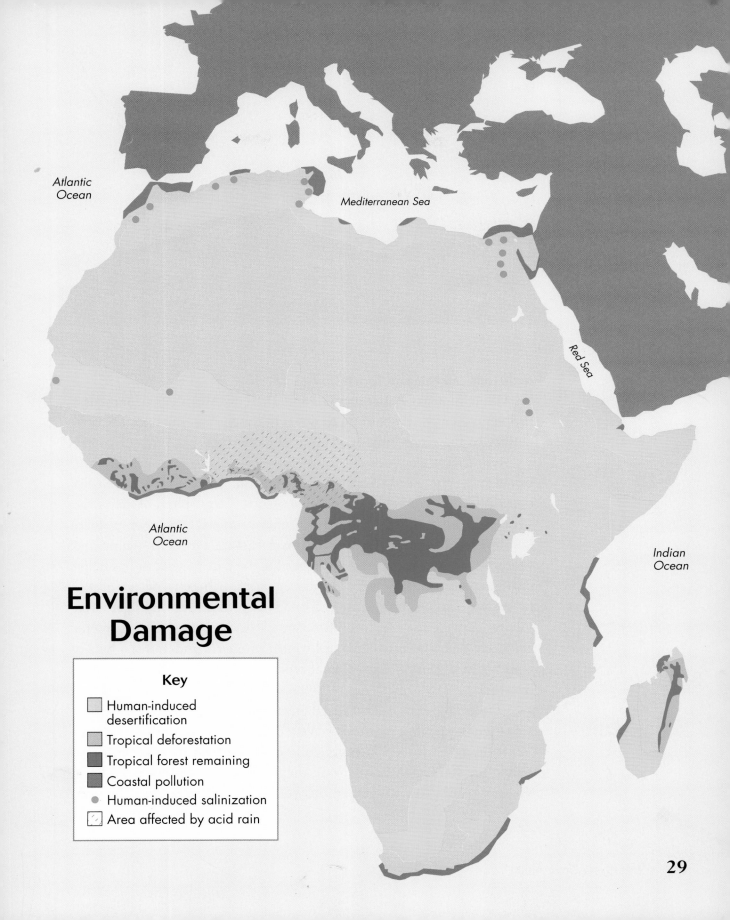

Atlantic
Ocean

Mediterranean Sea

Atlantic
Ocean

Red Sea

Indian
Ocean

Environmental
Damage

Key

- Human-induced desertification
- Tropical deforestation
- Tropical forest remaining
- Coastal pollution
- Human-induced salinization
- Area affected by acid rain

29

▶ *Right:* *The sand dunes that cross this road are dramatic evidence of desertification.*

The result has been the loss of vast acres of forest—and of many animals that call the rain forest home.

While industry has contributed its share to Africa's environmental problems—and will continue to do so in the future—it is not the only danger to the environment.

Rain forest trees are cut down not just for the lumber industry, but also for fuel, and to clear land for farming. Not only does this contribute to deforestation, it also worsens the problem of acid rain.

Desertification is another major environmental problem in Africa. It is a result of both natural and human forces. Drought—which has seriously affected some areas of Africa for the past 15 years—has helped change grassland to desert. Humans also contribute to desertification by the ways in which they use the land. As you can see on the environmental damage map featured on page 29, the most seriously affected areas are near the northern and southern coasts and along a belt of land north of central Africa, land typically used for raising crops and livestock.

One problem that has caused environmental damage has been a change in farming methods. With the traditional method, called "shifting agriculture," farmers cultivated the land in small areas. When the soil began to wear out, they moved to a new area and let the first place grow wild again before replanting. This gave the soil a chance to restore itself—to replace minerals and regain fertility. Modern farming methods call for farmers to stay in one place and cultivate a large area intensely for a long period of time. This has caused severe soil erosion and desertification.

Another cause of desertification has been overgrazing. In place of nomadic herding—moving cattle and sheep from one place to another to graze—there has been a trend toward establishing ranches, especially in southern Africa. Areas that are overgrazed eventually become covered with plants that livestock won't eat. These plants also don't return nutrients to the soil.

Salinization is yet another environmental problem that Africa faces. On some of the continent's major rivers, such as the Nile, dams have been built to control flooding and provide water for irrigation. In other areas, farmers have turned to irrigation in an attempt to increase their crop land. Unfortunately, some of these irrigation efforts have been so intensive that they have harmed the land they were supposed to help. Over-irrigation has caused salinization—a process in which the nutrients have been washed from the soil, leaving it crusted with salts. When this happens, the land becomes unfit for both crops and livestock. As you can see from the environmental damage map, salinization has occurred in parts of northern and central Africa.

A Closer Look

You can learn a lot about what a place is like by looking at different kinds of maps, one at a time. However, by comparing the information presented in two or more maps, you can discover something about how and why it got that way.

How does the physical map of Africa on page 10 help explain the location of many of the major cities, shown on the map of capitals and cities on page 35? Compare the two maps to find out. What other map or maps might be used to show why these cities are located where they are?

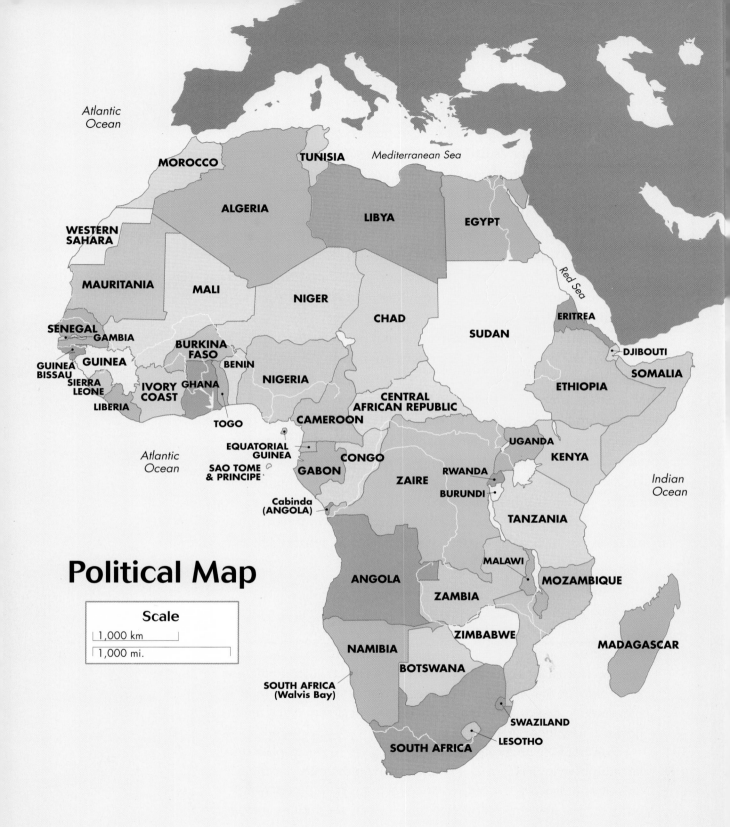

Political Map

Atlantic
Ocean

MOROCCO

TUNISIA

Mediterranean Sea

ALGERIA

LIBYA

EGYPT

WESTERN
SAHARA

MAURITANIA

MALI

NIGER

Red Sea

CHAD

SUDAN

ERITREA

SENEGAL
GAMBIA

GUINEA
BISSAU

GUINEA

BURKINA
FASO

BENIN

NIGERIA

DJIBOUTI

SIERRA
LEONE

IVORY
COAST

GHANA

CENTRAL
AFRICAN REPUBLIC

ETHIOPIA

SOMALIA

LIBERIA

TOGO

CAMEROON

Atlantic
Ocean

EQUATORIAL
GUINEA

CONGO

UGANDA

KENYA

SAO TOME
& PRINCIPE

GABON

ZAIRE

RWANDA

BURUNDI

Indian
Ocean

Cabinda
(ANGOLA)

TANZANIA

Scale

1,000 km

1,000 mi.

ANGOLA

MALAWI

MOZAMBIQUE

ZAMBIA

ZIMBABWE

MADAGASCAR

NAMIBIA

BOTSWANA

SOUTH AFRICA
(Walvis Bay)

SWAZILAND

LESOTHO

SOUTH AFRICA

Chapter 2

Mapping People, Cultures, and the Political World

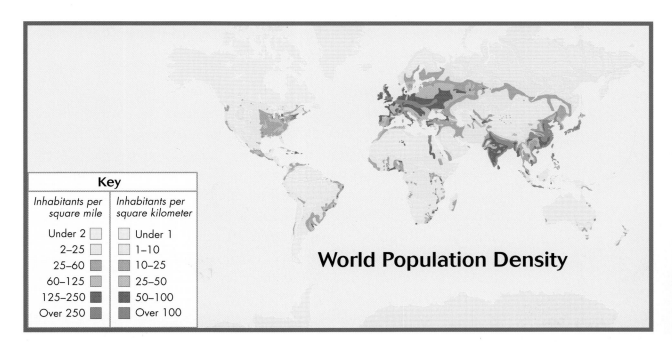

Key

Inhabitants per square mile	Inhabitants per square kilometer
Under 2	Under 1
2–25	1–10
25–60	10–25
60–125	25–50
125–250	50–100
Over 250	Over 100

World Population Density

Maps can reveal much more about a place than simply what it is like physically. They can also tell you a great deal about the political divisions of the area. Maps can inform you about the cultures and customs of the people who live there as well. They can show the languages spoken in a region, the religions people identify with, and the places where most people live.

▲ *Above:* Although Africa's population is thinnest in the hot deserts, in other parts of the world it is the coldest regions that have the fewest people.

◄◄ *Opposite:* The 53 nations of Africa all appear on this political map. See if you can find them.

The Political World: Dividing the Land

Political maps, such as the one of Africa on page 32, are familiar to everyone. In these, there is no attempt to show what an area physically looks like. Rather, a political map shows the boundaries that separate countries (or states and provinces). Colors are used to distinguish one country from another. A political map may also show capitals and major cities, as the map on the opposite page does.

Boundaries are artificial; that is, they are created, set, and changed by people. Conquests, wars, and treaties have all caused boundary changes. Political maps can, therefore, also be a guide to the history of a region.

Geographers keep track of boundary changes, and country and city name changes, as they occur, so that new, up-to-date political maps can be created as soon as possible.

Nature's Influence

The political world is not entirely separate from the natural world. Rivers or mountains may dictate where boundaries are set. Also, if there is a wealth of natural resources in one location, people may try to set boundaries that put all or most of those resources within their own country's borders. The location of cities is often influenced by natural features, as well. If you look at the map on the opposite page, and then at the physical map on page 10, you'll note that major cities tend to cluster along coastlines or major waterways. You will also find cities in areas that have less severe climates.

▶ **Right:** Aswan, Egypt, is one of the major cities along the picturesque Nile River, an important transportation route since ancient times.

▶▶ **Opposite:** Many of Africa's oldest cities, such as Alexandria, Egypt, and Casablanca, Morocco, are along the coast.

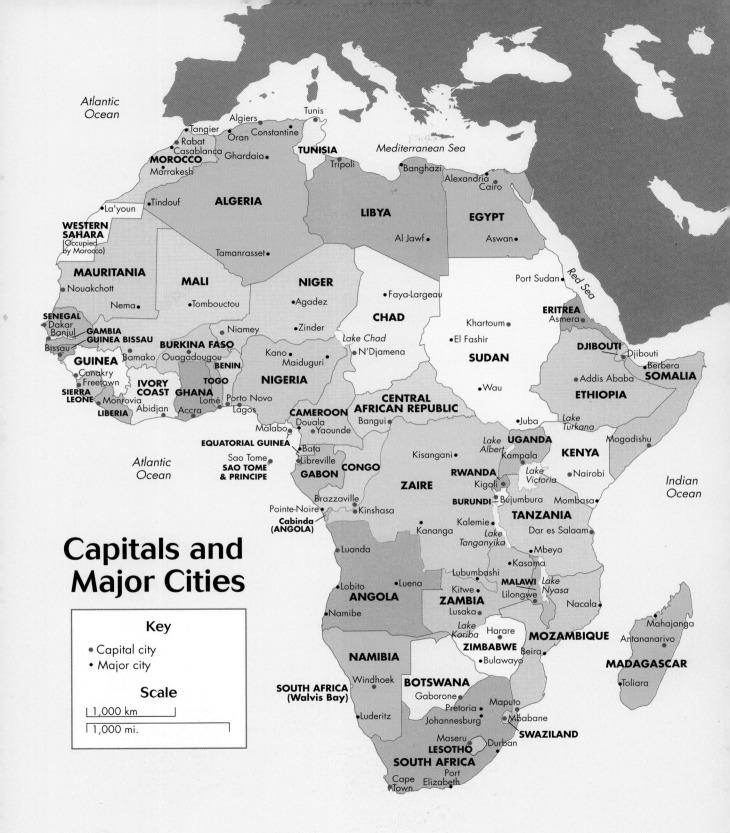

Capitals and Major Cities

Atlantic
Ocean

Tangier
Rabat
Casablanca
MOROCCO
Marrakesh

Algiers
Oran Constantine

TUNISIA

Tunis

Mediterranean Sea

Tripoli

Banghazi

Alexandria
Cairo

Ghardaia

La'youn

**WESTERN
SAHARA**
(Occupied
by Morocco)

Tindouf

ALGERIA

LIBYA

EGYPT

Al Jawf

Aswan

Tamanrasset

MAURITANIA

Nouakchott

MALI

Port Sudan

Red Sea

Nema

Tombouctou

NIGER

Faya-Largeau

Agadez

CHAD

Khartoum

ERITREA
Asmera

SENEGAL
Dakar
Banjul
GAMBIA
GUINEA BISSAU
Bissau

Niamey

Zinder

El Fashir

DJIBOUTI
Djibouti
Berbera

SUDAN

BURKINA FASO

Kano

Lake Chad
N'Djamena

GUINEA
Conakry
Freetown
**SIERRA
LEONE**
Monrovia

Bamako
Ouagadougou
BENIN
IVORY
COAST **GHANA**
Lomé
Abidjan Accra

Maiduguri

Wau

SOMALIA

Addis Ababa

ETHIOPIA

TOGO

NIGERIA
Porto Novo
Lagos

**CENTRAL
AFRICAN REPUBLIC**

Juba

Lake
Turkana

Mogadishu

LIBERIA

CAMEROON
Douala
Malabo Yaounde

Bangui

UGANDA
Kampala

Lake
Albert

KENYA

EQUATORIAL GUINEA
Bata
Sao Tome
Libreville
**SAO TOME
& PRINCIPE**

Kisangani

Nairobi

GABON

CONGO

ZAIRE

RWANDA
Kigali

Lake
Victoria

Atlantic
Ocean

Indian
Ocean

Brazzaville
Pointe-Noire
**Cabinda
(ANGOLA)**

Kinshasa

BURUNDI
Bujumbura

Mombasa

Kananga

Kalemie

TANZANIA

Dar es Salaam

Luanda

Lake
Tanganyika

Mbeya

Kasama

Lobito
Luena

Lubumbashi

Kitwe

MALAWI
Lilongwe

Lake
Nyasa

Nacala

ANGOLA

ZAMBIA
Lusaka

Mahajanga

Namibe

Lake
Kariba

Harare

MOZAMBIQUE

ZIMBABWE

Beira

Antananarivo

NAMIBIA

Bulawayo

MADAGASCAR

BOTSWANA

Windhoek

Gaborone

SOUTH AFRICA
(Walvis Bay)

Pretoria
Johannesburg

Maputo
Mbabane
SWAZILAND

Luderitz

Maseru
LESOTHO

Durban

Toliara

SOUTH AFRICA

Cape
Town

Port
Elizabeth

Key
- Capital city
- Major city

Scale
1,000 km
1,000 mi.

35

Africa's History and Political Divisions

A map drawn about A.D. 150 by Ptolemy, one of the first great map-makers, shows only the northern half of Africa in any kind of detail. The area below that is labeled *Terra Incognita*—"Unknown land." Even in the northern portion, it is the natural features, the rivers and lakes, that are carefully drawn in. The land itself is not separated by the political boundaries we are used to seeing on maps. But this doesn't mean that Africa wasn't already being divided up.

The division of Africa into its present 53 independent countries involves a long history of rising and falling kingdoms and city-states, European colonization, and struggles for independence and self-rule. The land has been divided up based on military power and on the urge to acquire economic power—to control valuable resources and trade.

Kingdoms and Empires

One of the world's first great civilizations, that of the Egyptians, arose along the Nile River around 3100 B.C. The kingdom of Kush, a center of learning and art—with an important iron industry—was established south of Egypt around 2000 B.C. By 30 B.C., the Roman Empire had conquered and controlled all of northern Africa along the Mediterranean.

Trade across the Sahara Desert brought power and prestige to cities located south of the Sahara in West Africa. Some of these cities grew into city-states, then kingdoms. Two of the most powerful West African kingdoms—Ghana and Mali—covered areas that now include Mauritania, Mali, Gambia, Guinea, and Senegal. Ghana was at its height of power around A.D. 1000, and Mali around A.D. 1200.

East coast cities below Africa's horn were founded as Arab trading settlements in the 1200s. (To find the horn, look for Somalia on the east coast.) Arab Muslims traded goods from India, China, and Indonesia for African gold and ivory. The Arabs also engaged the Africans in slave trading. Other large empires and kingdoms grew up in the central and southern parts of Africa during the 1400s.

Throughout this period, political boundaries changed with the rise and fall of power and wealth. Empires, kingdoms, and city-states grew and shrank in size with their importance. The most lasting land divisions were tribal. But boundaries were not yet drawn up on the sort of political-style map we are used to.

Portuguese Exploration

In the 1400s, the Portuguese began to explore Africa's west coast. They established trading forts along the coast to take advantage of Africa's gold and ivory resources.

At this time, too, Central and South America and the West Indies were being settled by Europeans, who were looking for laborers to work the new lands. Trading in slaves had been part of the north and east African economy for some time, but in a limited way. Now, slave trading began in earnest.

Slave Trading

Over the next 350 years, as plantation life became established in the Caribbean and in North America, European slave trading became big business. The African slave trade map on page 38 shows major slave trade routes during the period from 1601 to 1870. This was the height of the slave trade, when Dutch, British, and French traders

▼ *Below: Africans were forced into slavery for more than 350 years.*

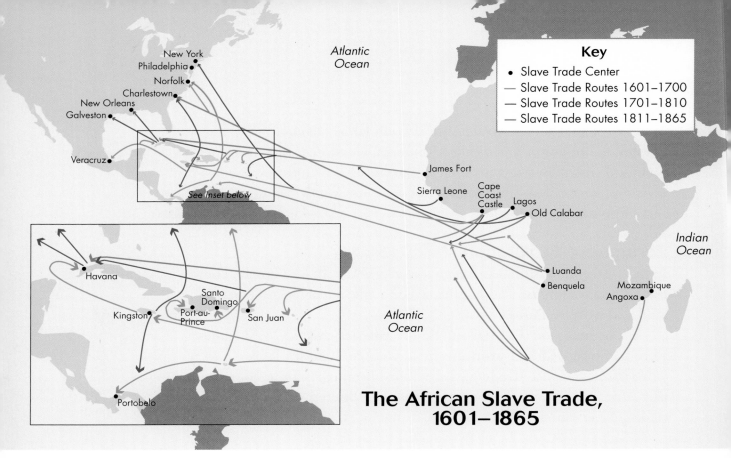

The African Slave Trade, 1601–1865

Key
- • Slave Trade Center
- — Slave Trade Routes 1601–1700
- — Slave Trade Routes 1701–1810
- — Slave Trade Routes 1811–1865

▲ **Above:** European traders sold African slaves to plantation owners in the Americas and West Indies (see inset) in exhange for goods.

joined the Portuguese. Although the map shows only the routes between Africa and the Americas, the third leg of this "triangle trade" was, of course, Europe.

Slave traders sailed from Europe to Africa, where they exchanged goods for people. These slaves were then taken to the Americas and sold to plantation owners. Finally, the slave traders returned to Europe carrying goods such as sugar, tobacco, and cotton with them. It has been estimated that 10 million slaves were brought to the Americas from Africa by the time slave trading declined in the late 1800s.

Colonial Rule

Although Europeans had explored and established settlements along the African coast for some time, it was not until the late 1700s that they began to move inland. Some explorers searched for the sources of major rivers such as the Nile and the Congo, others for the sources of minerals and other raw materials that they wanted for export and trade.

As the Europeans explored the interior of Africa, they mapped the areas they visited. They also wrote about and drew pictures of the things they saw. European exploration continued well into the 1800s. For example, British explorer Henry Stanley was traveling the Congo-Zaire River in the 1870s.

During this time—the 1700s to the late 1800s—large African kingdoms in the interior of the continent were still operating independently of European influence. In time, however, the European interest in establishing trade routes and settlements drastically changed the map face of Africa.

In 1884, in a meeting in Berlin, Germany, the European powers drew up an agreement that divided Africa among them. The divisions concentrated on resources, and were made without respect for tribal boundaries. This resulted in hard feelings because many tribes were split between two or more different countries, and freedom of movement was restricted. The Somali people, for example, found themselves divided among four countries: British Somaliland, French Somaliland, Italian Somaliland, and Ethiopia. (See the horn of Africa on the colonial map on page 40.)

With the 1884 agreement, political boundaries similar to modern-day boundaries appeared on the map of Africa for the first time. Over the next several years, shifts in these boundaries occurred through trade-offs and wars. As you can see from the map on page 40, by the time World War I began in 1914, European powers had colonized nearly all of Africa. If you compare this map to the political map on page 32, you'll notice that colonial Africa looked similar in 1920 to Africa today.

African Independence

Colonial rule dominated African life and economics until the 1960s. Although Europeans provided important medical and educational services, many Africans resented outsiders controlling their land and resources. Struggles to gain back their independence began almost

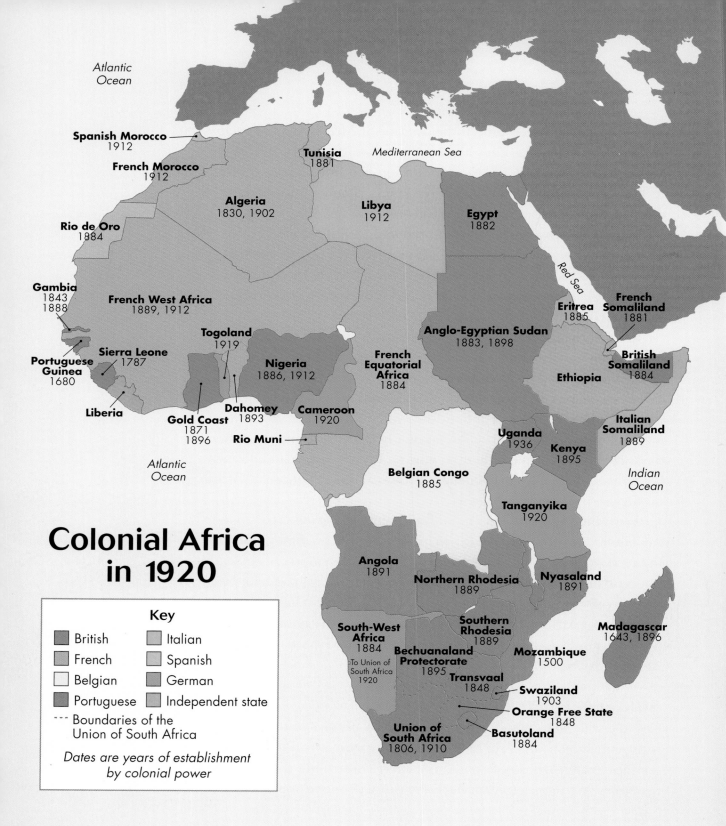

Atlantic
Ocean

Spanish Morocco
1912

French Morocco
1912

Rio de Oro
1884

Gambia
1843
1888

French West Africa
1889, 1912

Portuguese
Guinea
1680

Sierra Leone
1787

Liberia

Gold Coast
1871
1896

Togoland
1919

Dahomey
1893

Nigeria
1886, 1912

Rio Muni

Cameroon
1920

Tunisia
1881

Mediterranean Sea

Algeria
1830, 1902

Libya
1912

Egypt
1882

Red Sea

French
Equatorial
Africa
1884

Anglo-Egyptian Sudan
1883, 1898

Eritrea
1885

French
Somaliland
1881

British
Somaliland
1884

Ethiopia

Italian
Somaliland
1889

Uganda
1936

Kenya
1895

Belgian Congo
1885

Tanganyika
1920

Indian
Ocean

Atlantic
Ocean

Colonial Africa
in 1920

Angola
1891

Northern Rhodesia
1889

Nyasaland
1891

South-West
Africa
1884
To Union of
South Africa
1920

Bechuanaland
Protectorate
1895

Southern
Rhodesia
1889

Mozambique
1500

Madagascar
1643, 1896

Transvaal
1848

Swaziland
1903

Orange Free State
1848

Union of
South Africa
1806, 1910

Basutoland
1884

Key

British

French

Belgian

Portuguese

Italian

Spanish

German

Independent state

- - - Boundaries of the
Union of South Africa

*Dates are years of establishment
by colonial power*

immediately after colonization in some countries. The first African colony to gain independence was the Gold Coast. It gained its freedom from British rule in 1957, and took the name Ghana.

By the end of 1960, there were 27 independent African countries. By 1980, when Southern Rhodesia became Zimbabwe, there were 47 independent countries. South-West Africa, which became part of the Union of South Africa in 1920, gained its independence in 1990 and adopted the name Namibia. In 1993, Eritrea, which until then was considered a province of Ethiopia, formally gained its independence.

When they became free nations, many countries changed their names and some got new boundaries as well. But essentially, the map face of Africa remained remarkably the same as under colonial rule. Today, there are a number of civil wars—wars within countries— being fought. But these wars are more likely to bring about a change in governing powers than in country boundaries.

Population, Language, and Religion

Political maps tell us about the boundaries of a nation, but not about the lives of its inhabitants. Maps that focus on population, language, and religion tell us more about a country's people. Most national

◄◄ *Opposite: By 1920, very few African countries were independent. The dominant colonial powers were France and Great Britain.*

▼ *Below: Africa's population is growing more quickly than the populations of other continents.*

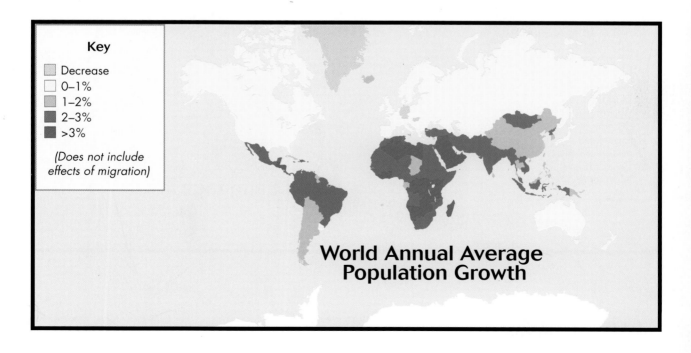

Key

Decrease
0–1%
1–2%
2–3%
>3%

(Does not include effects of migration)

World Annual Average Population Growth

governments conduct a census (population count) on some sort of regular basis. The United States, for example, has conducted a regular 10-year census since 1790. Census figures are used to make maps that show how population is distributed. The world population density map shown on page 33 is one such map. By compiling statistics over a period of years—from census and birth and death records—geographers can make predictions regarding population growth, as shown by the map on page 41.

Because many different languages may be spoken in any one country, it is difficult to map language distribution precisely. However, large areas that represent language families can be mapped, as shown in the world languages distribution map below. In the same way, predominant religions of an area can also be mapped, as shown in the world religions map on the opposite page. (This type of map does not show a region's minority religions, however.)

▼ **Below:** *Africa and Asia have the world's richest language distribution.*

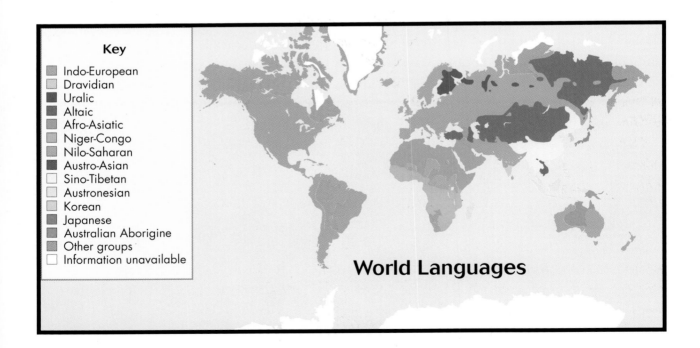

Key

- Indo-European
- Dravidian
- Uralic
- Altaic
- Afro-Asiatic
- Niger-Congo
- Nilo-Saharan
- Austro-Asian
- Sino-Tibetan
- Austronesian
- Korean
- Japanese
- Australian Aborigine
- Other groups
- Information unavailable

World Languages

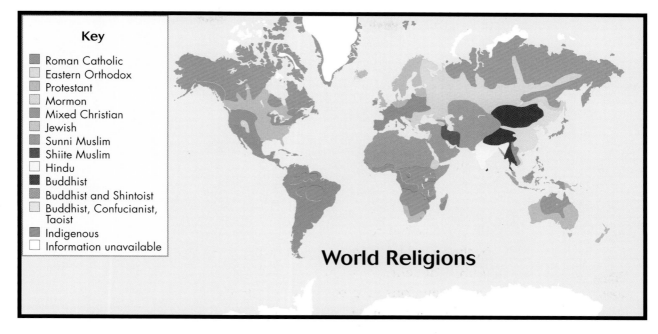

Key

- Roman Catholic
- Eastern Orthodox
- Protestant
- Mormon
- Mixed Christian
- Jewish
- Sunni Muslim
- Shiite Muslim
- Hindu
- Buddhist
- Buddhist and Shintoist
- Buddhist, Confucianist, Taoist
- Indigenous
- Information unavailable

World Religions

African Religions

Each African ethnic group has a traditional native religion of its own. These indigenous religions are practiced throughout Africa, but are especially important in some parts of central and southern Africa, as shown on the map on page 44. As you can see, Islam—specifically Sunni-Muslim— is the dominant religion in much of the continent, and it is on the increase.

Armies, missionaries, and traders have all played a part in establishing or spreading non-native religions throughout Africa. The Roman Empire brought Christianity to northern Africa in about A.D. 300. This lasted until the Arab Muslim empire established itself throughout northern Africa in the 600s, bringing the Islam religion to that area. Islam spread south across the Sahara into western and central Africa with trade caravans. Other Muslim traders, crossing the Indian Ocean, established Islam as the main religion along the eastern coast of Africa. Gradually, Islam became a major religious force throughout most of the continent, especially in northern Africa.

▲ *Above:* As you can see from this map, Europe and the Middle East is the only continent in the world where indigenous religions are not widely practiced.

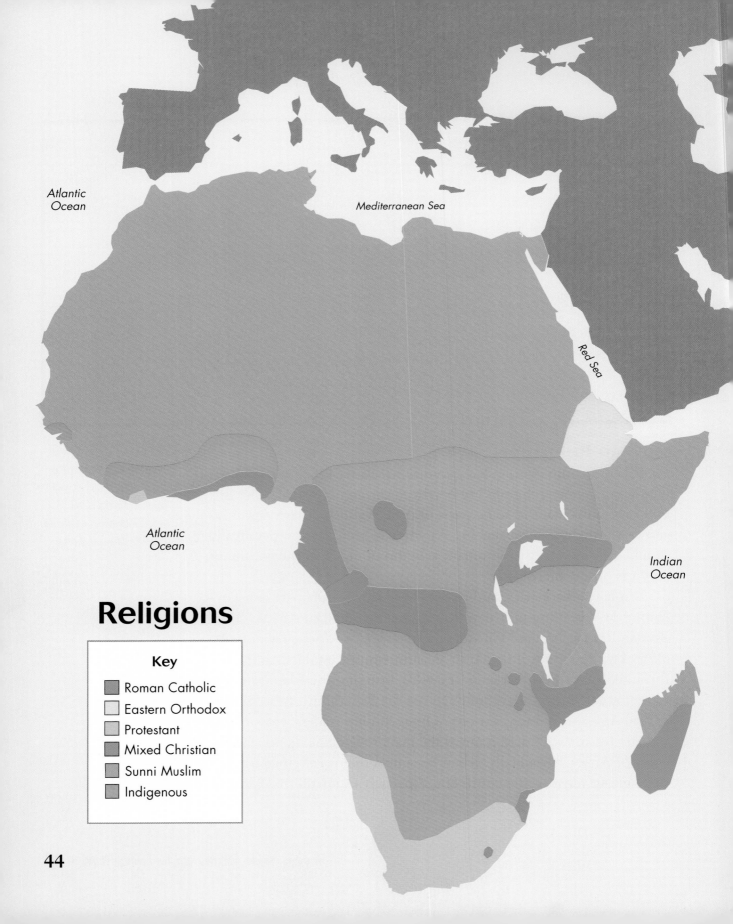

Atlantic
Ocean

Mediterranean Sea

Red Sea

Atlantic
Ocean

Indian
Ocean

Religions

Key

- ■ Roman Catholic
- □ Eastern Orthodox
- ■ Protestant
- ■ Mixed Christian
- ■ Sunni Muslim
- ■ Indigenous

Left: This Bedouin man praying in the desert is one of Africa's many Muslims.

Opposite: Although Christianity was the first nonindigenous religion to take hold in Africa, Islam—the religion of Sunnis and other Muslims—is more dominant.

Missionaries who accompanied European exploration of Africa in the 1700s and 1800s brought Christianity back to the continent. Dutch and English settlement in South Africa established a major Protestant presence there. Ethiopia has remained largely Eastern Orthodox throughout its history.

African Languages

The variety of languages spoken in Africa reflect the many ethnic groups that reside there. There are over 800 ethnic groups of native black Africans, each with its own distinct language. In addition, there are dialectical, or regional, languages. In all, more than 1,000 languages

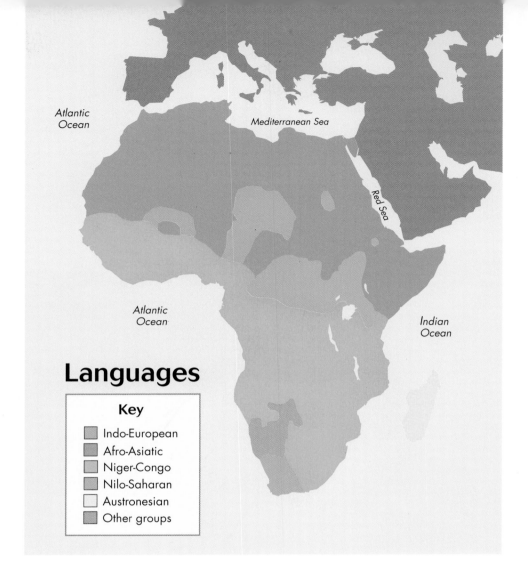

Languages

Key

- Indo-European
- Afro-Asiatic
- Niger-Congo
- Nilo-Saharan
- Austronesian
- Other groups

Atlantic
Ocean

Mediterranean Sea

Red Sea

Atlantic
Ocean

Indian
Ocean

▶ *Right:* *Among the "other groups" marked in brown on this languages map are the Khosian languages, spoken with a noticeable clicking sound.*

are spoken in Africa. The major languages can be roughly grouped as shown in the language distribution map above.

In the northern half of the continent, the primary group consists of Afro-Asiatic languages (shown in dark pink). Among these, the main languages are Berber and Arabic. The next-largest language group is Niger-Congo, in the west and the south. About 300 Bantu languages are included in this group, among them Swahili, the most widely spoken Bantu language.

As you can see by comparing the language distribution map and the political map on page 32, Nilo-Saharan languages are spoken in the areas of the central Sahara (Chad), Central African Republic,

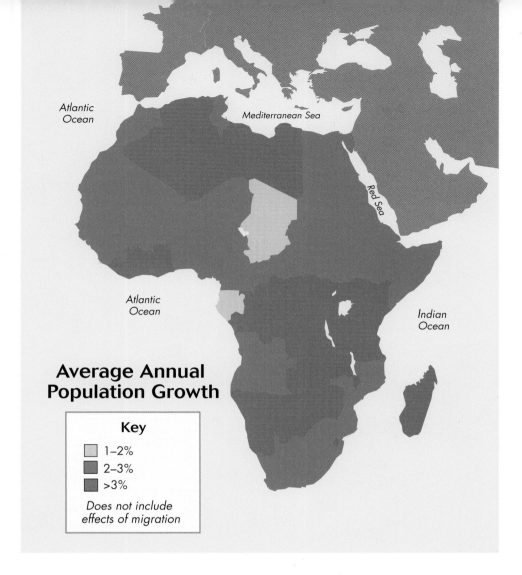

Average Annual Population Growth

Key

- 1–2%
- 2–3%
- >3%

Does not include effects of migration

Atlantic Ocean

Mediterranean Sea

Red Sea

Atlantic Ocean

Indian Ocean

◀ *Left:* Africa's population is growing rapidly.

parts of northern Zaire, southern Sudan, Uganda, and parts of Kenya and Tanzania, Mali, Niger, Nigeria, and Cameroon.

In the Cape area of South Africa, Indo-European English and Afrikaans, a Dutch-based language, are widely spoken. On the island of Madagascar, the primary language is Malagasy, an Austronesian language.

African Population Growth and Density

In 1950, the population of Africa was 224 million. By 1996, the population was estimated to be 731 million. In just 46 years, it had more than tripled.

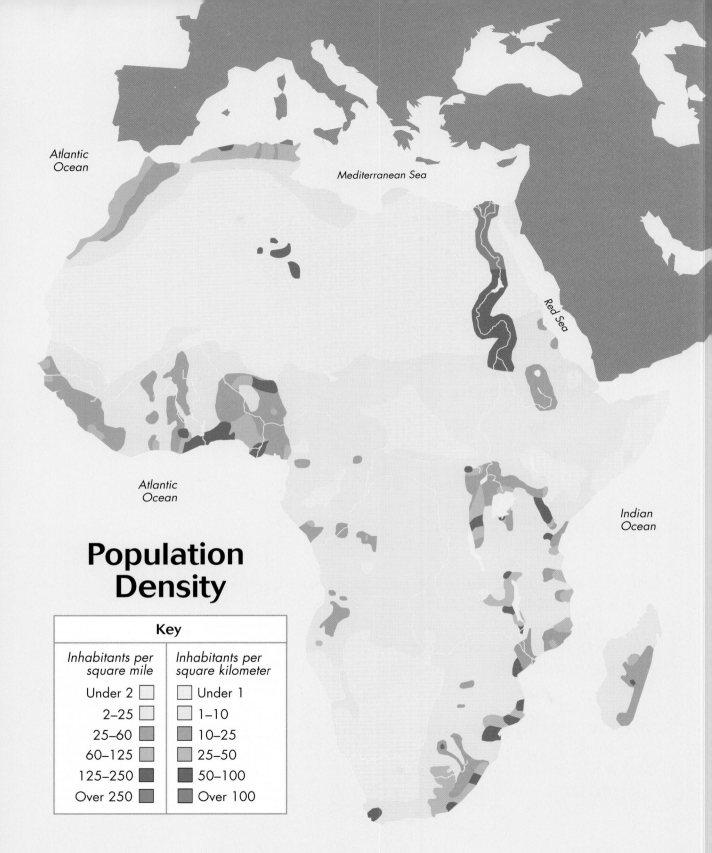

Population Density

Atlantic
Ocean

Mediterranean Sea

Red Sea

Atlantic
Ocean

Indian
Ocean

Key	
Inhabitants per square mile	Inhabitants per square kilometer
Under 2	Under 1
2–25	1–10
25–60	10–25
60–125	25–50
125–250	50–100
Over 250	Over 100

As you can see from the population growth map on page 47, most of the population increase has been south of the Sahara. Of the 731 million people living in Africa in 1996, about 597 million lived in this region. Africa's overall population is concentrated most heavily in just a few small areas. This is especially true in the north, which is mainly desert. If you look at the population density map on the opposite page, you will see that one major population center is found along the Nile River in Egypt. The Nile River valley is, in fact, one of the most heavily populated areas in the world. Other areas of Africa with extremely dense populations can be found along the Mediterranean coast in the northwest and along the coast between Ghana and Nigeria.

Because of drought and the rapidly expanded population, famine has become a major problem in Africa. In addition, more and more people are moving to the cities in an effort to find work. This has placed an enormous strain on the cities' resources, putting more pressure on the economy and the environment.

A Closer Look

Gross Domestic Product (GDP) is the total value of the output of a country—all products and labor. Dividing the value of a country's GDP by its population gives the per capita (per person) GDP. This figure represents the average annual income of that country's people.

In 1990, the per capita—per person—South African GDP was $5,500 in U.S. dollars. In Ethiopia, the per capita GDP was $120. By looking at the land use, mineral resources, and energy production maps in Chapter One, can you explain the income gap between South Africans and Ethiopians?

◀◀ *Opposite: Africa's population is very dense in some places along the coast and along the Nile River, and very thin in the deserts.*

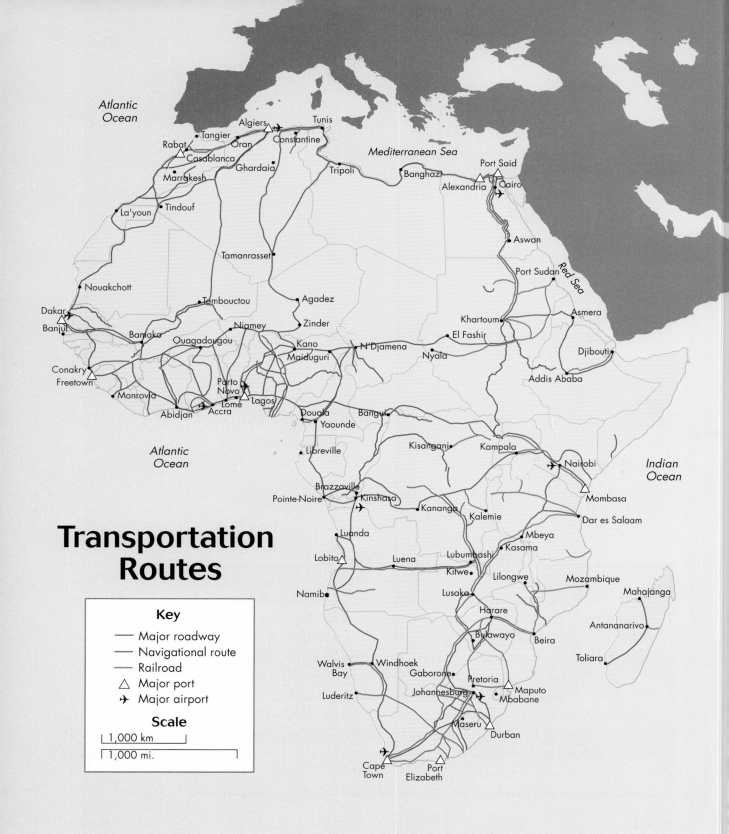

Transportation Routes

Atlantic Ocean

Mediterranean Sea

Red Sea

Atlantic Ocean

Indian Ocean

Tangier • Algiers • Tunis
Rabat • Oran • Constantine
Casablanca
Marrakesh • Ghardaia • Tripoli • Banghazi • Port Said
Alexandria • Cairo
La'youn • Tindouf
Aswan
Tamanrasset
Port Sudan
Nouakchott
Tombouctou • Agadez • Asmera
Dakar • Khartoum • El Fashir
Banjul • Bamako • Niamey • Zinder • N'Djamena • Nyala • Djibouti
Conakry • Ouagadougou • Kano • Addis Ababa
Freetown • Maiduguri
Monrovia • Porto Novo
Abidjan • Lomé • Lagos • Douala • Bangui
Accra • Yaounde
Libreville • Kisangani • Kampala • Nairobi
Mombasa
Brazzaville
Pointe-Noire • Kinshasa • Kananga • Kalemie • Dar es Salaam
Luanda • Mbeya • Kasama
Lobito • Luena • Lubumbashi
Kitwe • Lilongwe • Mozambique • Mahajanga
Namibe • Lusaka • Antananarivo
Harare • Beira • Toliara
Bulawayo
Walvis Bay • Windhoek • Gaborone
Luderitz • Johannesburg • Pretoria • Maputo • Mbabane
Maseru • Durban
Cape Town • Port Elizabeth

Key

— Major roadway
— Navigational route
— Railroad
△ Major port
✈ Major airport

Scale

⌐ 1,000 km ⌐
⌐ 1,000 mi. ⌐

3

Mapping the World Through Which We Move

In addition to showing us the physical and political characteristics of a country or a continent, maps can also have a more practical, "hands-on" purpose: They can assist us in moving through our world. Whether that world is an entire continent, a single city, or the second floor of an art museum, different maps provide us with the information we need to get from one point to another.

Maps Show the Way

Whenever we want to get from one place to another, maps can help us plan our routes by showing the options that are available. Maps show where roads are located and what kinds of roads they are. They can also tell us whether we can take an airplane, train, bus, or other form of transportation to get there. Once we reach our destination, maps again can help us plan how best to get around—on foot, by car, or by some kind of public transportation.

Creating Road and City Maps

To create road maps and city maps, mapmakers (cartographers) look first to base data maps that accurately position points to be included on

◀◀ *Opposite: Large portions of Africa have no major transportation routes. If you look at the climate zones map on page 15, you'll see that most of these places are in the desert.*

the new map. These base maps might be acquired from the federal government, states, or cities. Aerial photographs may be taken to show if, and how, any areas may have changed since the base map was made.

Then, cartographers contact agencies that can provide specific information about street names—the names that are used locally—that will be the most help to a person traveling in the area. Other agencies are contacted to determine which buildings or other points of interest are important and should be included on the map of the area. Field work—actually visiting the area being mapped—adds useful first-hand information.

The Importance of Scale

Choosing the right scale for a map is an important step in making sure that the map will be as useful as possible.

To help people find their way around downtown Boston, for example, a cartographer would design a large-scale map that gives a close-up view of all the streets. But suppose someone wanted to drive from Philadelphia, in eastern Pennsylvania, to Pittsburgh, in western Pennsylvania. Then a small-scale road map of the entire state would be more helpful than large-scale maps of all the cities between Philadelphia and Pittsburgh.

Scale also plays an important part in determining what is shown on a map. The smaller the scale, the more carefully cartographers must pick and choose the details that are being included. Careful selection is needed in order to keep a map from becoming too cluttered.

Transportation in Africa

A look at the map on page 50 shows that the major transportation routes in Africa tend to cluster along the edges of the continent. Few important roadways or rail lines cut across the interior of Africa. Those that do often follow long-established trade routes. For example, the roads that cross the Sahara were built along trans-Saharan caravan routes once traveled only by traders leading camel caravans across the desert.

Roads

Most of the roads in Africa today were built in the 1920s by the European colonial powers, who then brought trucks to the continent to transport goods. Each European country was most concerned with its own territory and trade. Therefore, the majority of roads were built to run within individual countries, rather than between them.

Of the more than 800,000 miles of roads in Africa, less than a tenth are paved. Paved roads often link capital cities with regional capitals, or provide transportation between the coast and plantations, mine sites, or industrial centers. In many areas, dirt or gravel roads become unusable during the rainy season, and even paved roads can become swamped.

Trucks and buses transport both goods and people on Africa's roadways. Most Africans do not own cars, and those who do live primarily in cities. Even in cities, however, the majority of people travel by bus, mini-bus, or taxi, as well as on foot.

Railroads

In the 1880s, Europeans who were exploring and colonizing Africa built railroads as a way to transport goods from the interior to the coasts for export. Many rail lines are still primarily used for freight. Organized rail systems are found mostly in northern Africa and South Africa, where, as you can see from the transportation routes map on page 50, there are more rail lines per square mile than in any other country in Africa. In other areas, linking separate rail lines to form an organized system can be a problem. Railroads, even within a single country, were often built to different gauges (widths), making them impossible to connect. Efforts are now being made to update Africa's road and rail systems.

Waterways

Africa's rivers provide important transportation routes inland. They have been less useful, however, for moving goods to the coasts because many rivers drop off into rapids or waterfalls as they near the coasts. As you can see from the transportation routes map on page 50, roads and rail lines help to link the navigable parts of major rivers (called "navigational routes" on the map), such as the Nile, Congo-Zaire, and Niger, to port areas.

Africa has few naturally indented, sheltered harbor areas because its coastline is so smooth. Where natural harbors do exist, such as at Mombasa on Kenya's east coast, the towns have served as major ports for hundreds of years. Alexandria has been arguably the continent's most important port for thousands of years.

Airlines

Because of Africa's large size and the lack of well-developed ground transportation systems, air travel is one of the best ways to get around the continent. Most African countries have their own airlines. These are used primarily for travel within or between countries rather than overseas. The "major airports" identified on the transportation routes map are those that are used extensively for overseas travel. If you look at the capitals and major cities map on page 35, you will see that all but one of the major airports is located in a capital city.

Other Transportation

Despite progress in rail and road improvement, walking and riding bicycles are still major forms of transport throughout Africa. Also, camels—while less important for transportation than they used to be—are still used in the Sahara.

The Cities of Africa

Take another look at the capitals and major cities map on page 35. You can easily see that most of the capitals and many of the major cities of Africa are located along the coast. Historically and geographically, this makes sense. Early explorers and traders established bases on the coastal plain because it was easier than advancing into the interior of the continent. Waterfalls, rapids, and other natural barriers blocked their way. But what about the important inland cities?

Look at the transportation routes map on page 50. Compare this map with the capitals and major cities map. Do you see that most of the important inland cities are located on major navigational routes? Comparing these two maps makes it easier to see why the capitals and major cities are located where they are.

Large African cities range in age from Alexandria—which dates from around 3100 B.C.—to those that were established during colonization in the late 1800s and early 1900s, such as Nairobi. The shape of the cities—how they are laid out—is influenced by who settled them and when, as well as why they were established.

Old cities that have grown significantly in modern times generally have two distinct sections: an old-town area with small buildings (both houses and businesses) crowded along narrow, twisting streets, and a modern section with large, new offices and commercial buildings set along wider, open streets. The wide streets were built to accommodate modern forms of transportation such as cars, trucks, and buses. Residential sections occupy separate areas outside the central business district. The streets of the modern section, or new town, are generally laid out in the orderly grid pattern typical of modern European cities.

Marrakesh

This kind of layout can be seen on the city map of Marrakesh, on the opposite page. This is the largest city in southern Morocco and a former capital. The *medina*, or old town, which dates from A.D. 1070, is located to the east. For protection against raiders, the city was surrounded by a wall (shown on the map by the toothed line). The word *bab* means "gate," and indicates a place at which there was a gate into the city, such as Bab Ksiba, in the south. The old palace grounds in the southeastern section of the city are also walled off, as the map shows. This was less for protection than for privacy—a sign of power and privilege.

The new town features broad avenues fanning out from the center, with other streets forming basically uniform rectangular or square patterns between the avenues.

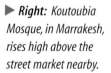

▶ *Right:* *Koutoubia Mosque, in Marrakesh, rises high above the street market nearby.*

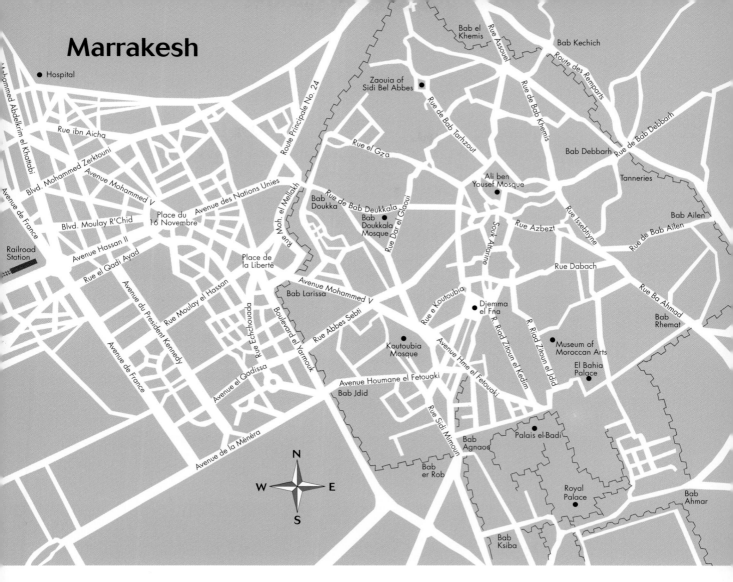

Marrakesh

- Hospital

Mohammed Abdelkrim el Khattabi

Rue ibn Aicha

Blvd. Mohammed Zerktouni

Avenue Mohammed V

Avenue de France

Blvd. Moulay R'Chid

Place du 16 Novembre

Avenue des Nations Unies

Avenue Hassan II

Rue el Qadi Ayad

Railroad Station

Place de la Liberté

Rue Moh. el Merlakh

Route Principale No. 24

Bab Doukka

Rue de Bab Deukkala

Bab Doukkala Mosque

Rue Dar el Glaoui

Avenue du President Kennedy

Rue Moulay el Hassan

Rue Echchouada

Boulevard el Yarmouk

Avenue Mohammed V

Bab Larissa

Rue Abbes Sebti

Avenue de France

Avenue el Qadissa

Koutoubia Mosque

Rue e Koutoubia

Avenue Hme el Fetouaki

Rue Sidi Mimoun

Avenue Houmane el Fetouaki

Bab Jdid

Avenue de la Ménéra

Bab er Rob

Bab Agnaou

Bab Ksiba

Zaouia of Sidi Bel Abbes

Rue de Bab Tarhzout

Rue el Gza

Rue de Bab Khemis

Ali ben Yousef Mosque

Souk Attarine

Rue Azbezt

Rue Dabach

Djemma el Fna

R. Riad Zitoun el Kedim

R. Riad Zitoun el Jdid

Museum of Moroccan Arts

El Bahia Palace

Palais el-Badi

Royal Palace

Bab el Khemis

Rue Assouel

Bab Kechich

Route des Remparts

Rue de Bab Khemis

Rue de Bab Debbarh

Bab Debbarh

Tanneries

Rue Issebfyne

Bab Ailen

Rue de Bab Ailen

Rue Ba Ahmad

Bab Rhemat

Bab Ahmar

N
W E
S

Most of Marrakesh's landmarks and tourist attractions are located in the old town. Koutoubia Mosque with its minaret (mosque tower) is a major attraction. This mosque, like most Muslim places of worship, is off-limits to non-Muslims. Its exterior, however, can be admired by all. Another special attraction is the ruins of the old palace—the Palais el-Badi.

Activity in the old town centers around the Djemma el Fna, an open area crowded with market stalls and street performers. To the north is a section filled with souks—market areas with narrow, twisting streets, each filled with shops that specialize in certain goods.

▲ **Above:** *The winding roads of the old section of Marrakesh, inside the city's walls, contrast sharply with the more regularly laid out roads of the city's modern section.*

Nairobi

Nairobi is the largest city in East Africa, and it has a very modern look. The main, central portion of the city is completely grid designed. Nairobi was originally a railroad camp, set up in 1896, when the British were building a rail line from the Kenyan capital of Mombasa, on the coast, to the highlands. By 1907, the railroad camp town had grown into a city big enough to replace Mombasa as the capital of Kenya.

Among the landmarks in the southern half of Nairobi's city center is the 28-story Kenyatta Conference Centre, the tallest building in the city. The captivating Parliament House can be recognized by its clock tower. The parliament buildings are decorated with African art, including a display of huge African sculptures. Nearby is the mausoleum where Jomo Kenyatta is buried. Kenyatta became Kenya's first president when the country won independence from Great Britain in 1963.

▼ *Below:* Nairobi is one of Africa's major urban centers.

A major landmark in the northern half of the central city is Jamia Mosque, built in 1925. Here, too, you'll find the City Market and its surrounding market stalls.

▲ *Above: Nairobi's streets are laid out in a modern grid.*

Other Maps and Guides

In addition to road and city street maps, there are many other maps and guides that are useful to us in moving through our world. There are navigational charts for boaters and maps that show special points of interest, such as all the caves in a state or all the parks or monuments in a city. Floor plans that guide you through famous buildings and museums are another kind of map. And there are trail guides for hikers, bikers, skiers, and horseback riders.

However you choose to get around our vast and complicated world—and wherever you choose to go—you will always find that maps will help you do it much more easily.

Africa's Pyramids and Parks

Among the biggest tourist attractions in Africa are the remnants of the ancient Egyptian civilization of the Nile and the many national parks and game reserves of East Africa. Many maps are available to introduce visitors to these African wonders, and to help make a trip to the continent easier and more enjoyable.

For example, the map below shows the typical floor plan of an ancient Egyptian mortuary (burial) temple. Maps such as this, prepared by archaeologists and historians, can help introduce you to the history and customs of ancient civilizations.

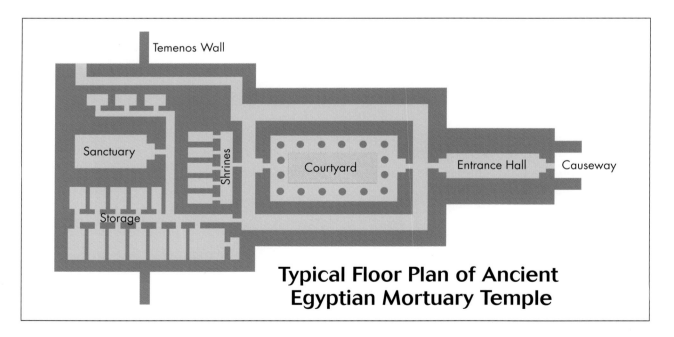

Temenos Wall

Sanctuary

Shrines

Courtyard

Entrance Hall

Causeway

Storage

Typical Floor Plan of Ancient Egyptian Mortuary Temple

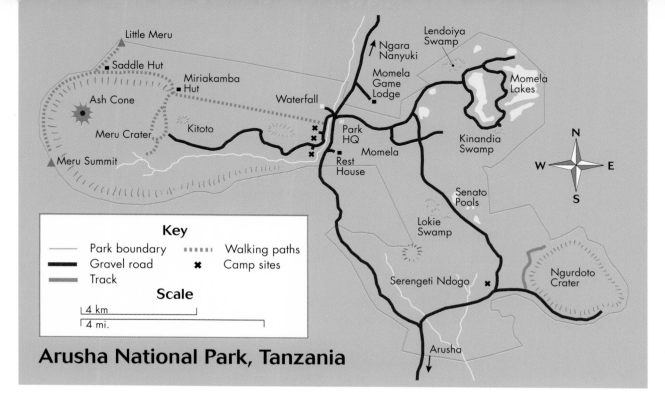

Arusha National Park, Tanzania

When it comes to exploring the natural world of modern-day Africa, maps such as the one above are helpful. This map not only sets out the various ways to get around Arusha National Park (roads and walking paths), but also shows places to camp and lodge. Details are provided to show various natural features found in the park, such as the ash cone left by an old volcano. Specialized guidebooks would, of course, provide additional information, as would maps regarding these and other tourist attractions.

▲ *Above: Africa's parks and preserves are so large that maps like this one are essential.*

A Closer Look

When we map the world through which we move, many of the maps—such as road and city maps—are especially designed to give us a closer look at a place. They tell us how to get around or what we can expect to see in a particular place.

Look at the maps of Marrakesh and Nairobi. Where do you think it would be easiest to find your way around? Why? Plan a tour of one city. Choose a starting point, then write out the route you would take to visit at least four attractions. Look at the the area the map covers. Do you think your tour would be a walking tour, or would you have to use a car or bus to get around?

Glossary

acid rain Rain that has collected waste gases from the atmosphere and is damaging to the environment.

cash crop A crop that is grown to be sold.

colonization Occupying another country to use its resources.

deforestation Large-scale clearing of forested land, which may die as a result.

delta A triangle-shaped area where a river deposits silt (fine grains of soil) before entering a sea or ocean.

desertification The creation of desert conditions as a result of long droughts, overgrazing, or soil erosion.

drought A long period without rainfall.

erosion Wearing away by the action of wind or water.

export Something sold and shipped to another country.

gross domestic product (GDP) The total output of a country; all products and labor.

hardwood Broadleaf trees (see **softwood**).

indigenous Original to a particular place.

oasis (plural, oases) A fertile area in a desert.

per capita Per person (literally, "per head").

plateau A large, mostly level, area of land that is higher than the land surrounding it.

salinization The process by which nutrients are washed from the soil by over-irrigation, leaving the soil encrusted with salts.

shifting agriculture Farming a small area of land until the soil is nearly worn out, then moving on, leaving the first area to grow wild and renew itself naturally.

softwood Coniferous, or cone-bearing, trees.

subsistence farming Growing crops or raising animals for personal use, rather than for sale or trade.

Further Reading

Africa. Vol. 1 of *Lands and Peoples*. Danbury, CT: Grolier Inc., 1997.

Encyclopedia of World Geography. Vols. 16, 17, & 18. New York: Marshall Cavendish Corporation, 1994.

Halliburton, Warren J. *City and Village Life*. New York: Crestwood House, 1993.

Ibazebo, Isimeme. *Exploration Into Africa*. New York: New Discovery Books, 1994.

Murray, Jocelyn. *Africa*. New York: Facts On File, Inc., 1990.

National Geographic Picture Atlas of Our World. Washington, D.C.: National Geographic Society, 1991.

Index